Managi **aching**

This book, *Managing Effective Learning and Teaching*, is a core text for the module 'Managing the curriculum' of the MBA in educational management offered by the Centre for Educational Leadership and Management (CELM), formerly the EMDU, University of Leicester. It is also a core text for the MA module 'Managing effective learning and teaching.'

The modules in the MBA in educational management are:

Leadership and Strategic Management in Education
Managing Finance and External Relations
Human Resource Management in Schools and Colleges
Managing the Curriculum
Research Methods in Educational Management

For further information about the MBA in educational management, please contact the CELM at celm@le.ac.uk. For further information about the books associated with the course, contact Paul Chapman Publishing at www.paulchapmanpublishing.co.uk

Educational Management Research and Practice series

Managing People in Education (1997)
    edited by Tony Bush and David Middlewood
Strategic Management in Schools and Colleges (1998)
    edited by David Middlewood and Jacky Lumby
Managing External Relations in Schools and Colleges (1999)
    edited by Jacky Lumby and Nick Foskett
Practitioner Research in Education (1999)
    by David Middlewood, Marianne Coleman and Jacky Lumby
Managing Finance and Resources in Education (2000)
    edited by Marianne Coleman and Lesley Anderson
Managing the Curriculum (2001)
    edited by David Middlewood and Neil Burton
Managing Further Education – Learning Enterprise (2001) by Jacky Lumby

Course books

Human Resource Management in Schools and Colleges (1999)
    by David Middlewood and Jacky Lumby
Leadership and Strategic Management in Education (2000)
    by Tony Bush and Marianne Coleman
Managing Finance, Resources and Stakeholders in Education (2001)
    by Lesley Anderson, Ann R.J. Briggs and Neil Burton

University *of*
Leicester

Managing Effective Learning and Teaching

Ann R.J. Briggs and
Daniela Sommefeldt

SAGE Publications
London • Thousand Oaks • New Delhi

First published 2002 under the Paul Chapman Publishing imprint.

Reprinted 2003, 2006 (twice)

SAGE Publications Ltd.
1 Oliver's Yard, 55 City Road
London EC1Y 1SP

SAGE Publications Inc
2455 Teller Road
Thousand Oaks, California 91320

SAGE Publications India Pvt Ltd.
B-42 Panchsheel Enclave
Post Box 4109
New Delhi 100 017

Library of Congress Control Number: 2002104966

A catalogue record for this book is available from the British Library

ISBN 10: 0-7619-4783-3
ISBN 10: 0-7619-4784-1 (pbk)
ISBN-13: 978-0-7619-4783-7
ISBN-13: 978-0-7619-4784-4 (pbk)

Typeset by Pantek Arts Ltd., Maidstone, Kent
Printed and bound in Great Britain by
Athenaeum Press Ltd., Gateshead, Tyne & Wear.

Contents

The authors

Ann Briggs and **Daniela Sommefeldt** both work in the Centre for Educational Leadership and Management (CELM), formerly EMDU of the University of Leicester.

Ann Briggs is a lecturer in educational management in the CELM. She has considerable experience of secondary and further education, including a range of middle management posts. She has contributed to *Managing Finance and Resources in Education* (2000), *Managing the Curriculum* (2001) and *Research Methods in Educational Leadership Management* (2002) – of which she is co-editor with Marianne Coleman – all in the *Educational Management: Research and Practice* series, published by Paul Chapman. She is co-author with Lesley Anderson and Neil Burton of *Managing Finance, Resources and Stakeholders in Education*, a companion text to this volume.

Daniela Sommefeldt is a senior tutor in educational management in the CELM. She has taught in both primary and secondary schools, although the greater part of her teaching has been in special education, working in schools for children with severe and profound learning difficulties. She was a headteacher for 17 years. She has contributed to *Managing the Curriculum* (2001). She also works with aspiring headteachers through NPQH and, with new headteachers, through Headlamp.

Acknowledgements

We would like to acknowledge the authors of the previous edition of this text: Mark Lofthouse, Tony Bush, Marianne Coleman, John O'Neill, John West-Burnham and Derek Glover.

We would like to acknowledge material provided by Lorna Unwin and Joseph Wong.

We also thank academic staff at EMDU for their help in the planning and development of this book, and Pip Murray for her administrative support and work on the manuscript.

Finally, thanks go to Christopher Bowring-Carr for preparing the index.

Introduction

This book is intended primarily for students on postgraduate courses in educational management, in particular for the University of Leicester's MBA in educational management, offered by its Centre for Educational Leadership and Management. It is therefore written as a text for study. However, it is also offered as a useful reference book for those working in a range of educational settings, offering an opportunity to increase their knowledge, understanding and skills in aspects of educational management.

The specific aims of this book are to:

- Equip the readers with a body of knowledge that will improve their understanding of curriculum, learning and teaching

- Enable readers to reflect on concepts, theories and models of curriculum management in education

- Provide a range of analytical frameworks that can be applied by readers to their own working environments

- Provide opportunities for the improvement of their skills in managing learning, teaching and the curriculum through site-based research

- Enable readers to contribute to school or college improvement in its management of the curriculum.

By the end of this book, readers should be able to:

- Set their own knowledge of learning, teaching and the curriculum in a wider context of theory and practice through an awareness of relevant literature in the field

- Clarify the linkages between theory, values and strategies in the management of learning, teaching and the curriculum in their own school or college situation

- Analyse critically their own institution's current practice in the management of learning, teaching and the curriculum

- Apply concepts of learning, teaching and curriculum management to their own management practice.

❑ Activities
Throughout the book you will find activities that ask you to:

- Analyse and reflect on what you have read
- Examine and criticise practice constructively
- Develop explanations to test the relationship between theory and practice.

These activities help you to consider what you have read and to relate it to your own management practice, now and in the future. They may assist you when you are considering a specific topic to include for a written assignment.

❑ Linked reading
The text is free-standing and contains ample material for the reader to be able to improve his or her management practice or produce a course assignment or project. However, additional material is clearly helpful and, for students, essential. There are two key books to draw to your attention:

1. Middlewood, D. and Burton, N. (eds) (2001) *Managing the Curriculum*. London: Paul Chapman. All the chapters in this volume are relevant to your study and you will be asked to read certain chapters at specific points in the text.

2. Bush, T. and Bell, L. (eds) (2002): *The Principles and Practice of Educational Management*. London: Paul Chapman. The following chapters are particularly relevant to this book: Chapter 4 'Leadership and strategy' by Cheng Yin Cheong; Chapter 9 'Managing for equal opportunities' by Marianne Coleman; Chapter 10 'Managing a prescribed curriculum' by Margaret Preedy; Chapter 11 'Monitoring and evaluating learning' by Ann Briggs; Chapter 17 'Managing organisational change to improve teaching and learning' by Hugh Busher; and Chapter 18 'External evaluation and inspection' by Brian Fidler.

❑ Structure of this book

This book in presented in three main chapters, each of which underpins the understanding of curriculum management in schools and colleges and the management of effective learning and teaching. In the first we explore the concept of curriculum and examine the forces that shape it in a range of contexts and countries. We draw the link between curriculum and pedagogy, which leads to a consideration of the relationship between managing the curriculum itself and managing the activities of learning and teaching. In this section we also consider the ways in which institutional values and issues of equity affect the management of teaching and learning.

In the second chapter we consider the implications for management of the contexts for learning and teaching. Learning styles and teaching strategies are explored through a discussion of theory and practice. Learning is then considered within its setting – in the classroom, beyond the school or college and in the 'virtual classroom' – to explore ways in which the learning environment may be managed to enable effective teaching and learning to take place.

Thirdly, we consider the responsibilities of people who manage learning and teaching. School and college structures are discussed, leading to a discussion of a range of curriculum management roles. The management of the learning process – planning, assessment, monitoring, evaluation – is examined in order to identify models of good practice. Finally, we turn to the consideration of the management of change: a responsibility often undertaken by those with curriculum responsibilities.

The book concludes by bringing the focus back to the learner, as a reminder of the primary purpose of the management processes discussed in the book.

❑ Note

In this text we refer to institutions of non-advanced post-compulsory education generically as 'colleges'. Worldwide, the name of this type of institution varies, but terminology includes technical colleges, further education colleges, vocational schools and community colleges. We do not specifically include universities in this category, but many of the concepts offered here would apply also to universities.

1. The rationale for learning

This chapter considers:

- **Introduction**
- **Defining the curriculum**
- **Constructing a national curriculum**
  - international curriculum models
- **Framing the curriculum for learning and teaching**
  - lifelong learning
  - curriculum models
  - the prescribed curriculum
- **Curriculum control**
  - the role of the state
  - the role of stakeholders
- **Institutional values, culture and ethos**
  - institutional culture and the hidden curriculum
- **Issues of equity**
- **The changing pedagogy**

Introduction

In this chapter you will be introduced to some of the key concepts that underpin the study of *learning*. In order to achieve a better understanding of learning, as this term is applied to what happens in schools and colleges (and beyond), we will look at the curriculum, teaching and learning from a number of perspectives, as indicated above.

The *curriculum* is a blanket term that is used to describe anything and everything that goes on in a school or college, including teaching and learning. We talk of curriculum planning and design, curriculum delivery, curriculum development, curriculum management and so on; these terms are shorthand for a complex set of ideas and practices that underpin and support the learning process. The curriculum may be seen as the framework within which teaching and learning take place. By increasing our understanding of this framework, we are able to reflect upon both our own practice and on the systems in place within our institutions.

Teaching and learning do not take place within a vacuum and the influences at work inside and outside formal education will affect what is taught and how learning may take place. The choices that have to be made are many and complex, ranging from who is given access to education to what is the best education possible. We will examine some of the major influences at work in the modern world in order to try to understand the context within which we now operate.

Defining the curriculum

At the heart of any discussion of the curriculum is the problem of how it may be defined. The etymology of the word *curriculum* derives from the Latin for *racing chariot*, which suggests the notion of a racetrack and a course to be run, which in turn leads us to the idea of a course of study. The concept of curriculum does not, as we shall see, simply equate to a course of study, although *syllabus*, which does relate more closely to this derivation, is often used interchangeably with curriculum. Kelly (1999) sees this confusion of terms as limiting: syllabus is a piecemeal rather than an overall view of the total curriculum. He goes on to say (2000, p. 3):

> Any definition of curriculum, if it is to be practically effective and productive, must offer much more than a statement about the knowledge-content or merely the subjects which schooling is to 'teach' or transmit. It must go far beyond this to an explanation, and indeed a justification, of the purposes of such transmission and an exploration of the effects that exposure to such knowledge and such subjects is likely to have, or is intended to have, on its recipients . . .

Philosophers over the centuries have debated the nature and purpose of education in its broadest sense. From earliest times, attempts have been made to define both the purpose and structure of education, as well as what constitutes an appropriate curriculum. In Ancient Greece, Aristotle, for example, argued for a rationale to be developed, which strikes chords for modern educators. He is clear on the context of education, but poses questions about the nature of the curriculum and the way it should be taught, as this passage clearly illustrates:

> It is clear then that there should be legislation about education and that it should be conducted on a public system. But consideration must be given to the question, what constitutes education and what is the proper way to be educated. At present, there are differences of opinion as to the proper tasks to be set; for all peoples do not agree as to the things that the young ought to learn, either with a view to virtue or with a view to the best life, nor is it clear whether their studies should be regulated more with regard to intellect or with regard to character. And confusing questions arise out of the education that actually prevails, and it is not at all clear whether the pupils should practise pursuits that are practically useful, or morally edifying, or higher accomplishments – for all these views have won the support of some judges; and nothing is agreed as regards the exercise conducive to virtue, for, to start with, all men do not honour the same virtue, so that they naturally hold different opinions in regard to training in virtue (Aristotle, *Politics*, Book 8).

Aristotle describes the four 'customary subjects of education' as reading and writing, gymnastics, music and drawing, although he is at pains to explain the distinctions between how these subjects may be applied to what he calls the 'first principle of leisure'. With the possible exception of Aristotle's assertion that 'leisure is a more desirable and more fully an end than business', there seems little in his argument that does not apply equally to modern curriculum debate. We should remember, of course, that Aristotle, when reflecting upon an appropriate curriculum for the young, did have in mind only upper-class males.

In this book we will present a number of definitions of the curriculum; the following example, from Ross (2000) is a recent interpretation, which provides a picturesque view of curriculum design. Ross (2000., p. 2) echoes the views of many educational philosophers when he defines the curriculum as 'a social construct open to criticism and analysis'. As an introductory example, we look at Ross's memorable image of four forms of curriculum, which he likens to types of garden (an ingenious and entertaining analogy). These are as follows:

1. *Baroque* As in the formal garden, this type of curriculum contains clearly demarcated subjects, classified by content knowledge and by discourse forms specific to each discipline. He references Bernstein's view that the learner has little control over selection, organisation and pacing of transmission of knowledge.

2. *Naturally landscaped* Here there are weak boundaries; the curriculum is governed by the nature of the learner. Subjects are artificial, dividing knowledge with contrived distinctions of process, knowledge and procedures. Rousseau's *Emile* is used as an example, where education is based on the child's unfolding nature within meaningful contexts. This sees the teacher as gardener and thus what appears to be a spontaneous unfolding of nature is ultimately contrived.

3. *Dig-for-victory* Taking as its starting point the World War II exhortation to turn over flower gardens to food production, this is a utilitarian concept. The learner is prepared for future roles in work and society, developing the relationship between schooling and industry by teaching workforce skills. The emphasis is on modes of learning that promote skills acquisition through learning objectives and predictable outcomes.

4. *Cottage garden* A quintessentially English notion, which encompasses a mixed planting. The curriculum conserves unchanging elements with new innovations (intended or otherwise). There are competing claims, leading to bargaining and negotiation rather than evolution and change.

Activity

How does your garden grow?

Before going on to read about how the curriculum has been constructed in different societies, take a little time to consider how your own school or college curriculum may be defined. Using the analogy of the garden, how would you describe the curriculum?

If you are not a gardener, you may prefer to choose a different analogy that has more appeal for you – the curriculum as types of car, perhaps? For example, the old banger, the sleek sports car, the family saloon, the zippy runaround . . .

❏ Our comments

Perhaps you tend a market garden, nurturing those characteristics that will find willing buyers, or maybe your curriculum garden is choked with weeds, allowing only the strongest of students to find those elements they need to survive? As a teacher-gardener, do you subscribe to the organic approach, which requires labour-intensive cultivation methods, or are you in favour of controlled planting, using the available technology to keep your garden weed and pest free?

Grasping the concept of what curriculum means in its totality is not easy and teachers will often be happy with a good 'working definition' that meets their immediate needs. However, in order to develop a deeper understanding of learning and teaching it is important to consider how and why education, as exemplified by what we call curriculum, has evolved into its present form. In the next section you will read about social theories that underpin curriculum development and how these theories are translated into practice. We will also consider how national and local curriculum models are being influenced by global trends.

Constructing a national curriculum

As can be seen from the examples given above, posing questions about the nature of the curriculum, or describing different types of curriculum, may be easier to achieve than a clear definition that encompasses all we mean by the term. The curriculum has meant different things to different people at different times in human history. A widely held view (e.g. Bernstein, 1971; Lawton, 1996) is that the curriculum is a social construct, designed to transmit the characteristics of the society it is designed to serve from one generation to another. A society maintains and develops its identity over time through a continuous defining and redefining of its particular culture within the context of an ever-changing world. The effects of globalisation on different cultures may mean the curriculum is starting to acquire familiar characteristics across and within societies, but national and local idiosyncrasies are still crucial in the development of curriculum theory and practice. In this section we will consider some of the major ideas in this area.

Lawton (1996, p. 26) describes how a cultural analysis will assist in curriculum planning and identifies the questions that will inform this analysis:

- What kind of society already exists?
- In what ways is it developing?
- How do its members appear to want it to develop?
- What kinds of values and principles will be involved in deciding on this development, as well as the educational means of achieving it?

A good starting point is to think about how the culture in question has developed to where it is now, to develop an historical perspective. Lawton suggests three kinds of classification are needed to help us examine a culture in detail. He requires us to define the major parameters of the culture; by this he means those cultural invariants or human universals that apply. The next step would be to outline a method of analysis to describe how societies make use of those parameters. Finally, a means of classifying the 'educationally desirable knowledge and experiences' is required. A simple model (Figure 1.1) is proposed, which Lawton offers as a guide to action at any level of curriculum planning, from national guidelines to lesson preparation by individual teachers.

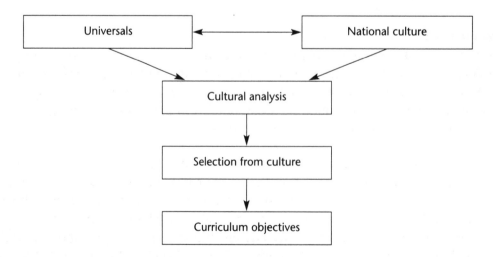

Figure 1.1 Curriculum – selecting from the culture
Source: Adapted from Lawton (1996, p. 26)

Lawton goes on to identify nine cultural invariants, or subsystems, which are universal to all societies. He makes the point that some of them may be more important than others in terms of their impact on formal education in some societies than in others. The systems identified are as follows:

1. Socio-political system (*this is closely related to 2 and 5*)

2. Economic system (*simple through to complex*)

3. Communications system (*speech, signs, symbols, signalling*)

4. Rationality system (*rules and explanations*)

5. Technology system (*simple tools through to complex electronics*)

6. Morality system (*codes of behaviour – unitary and pluralistic*)

7. Belief system (*religious/secular – related to 6 and 4*)

8. Aesthetic system (*the arts – simple to sophisticated*)

9. Maturation system (*child-rearing practices – transition to adulthood*).

The society must have some means of transmitting its unique characteristics from one generation to another. Formal schooling, possibly supported by other agencies such as the family or organised religion, is the obvious medium for this transmission in most countries across the world.

International curriculum models

It may be useful at this point to try to identify what are the educational commonalities across cultures and societies as well as to consider what differences can and do exist within the context of the global knowledge exchange permitted by technology such as the Internet. Ross (2000) describes how George Meyer's team at Stanford University has examined curriculum categories at the primary level in over 70 countries since the 1920s. Whilst accepting that the data are limited and should be interpreted with caution, Meyer believes some homogeneity has been found across countries. The broad similarities seem to outweigh the differences; local national variations have been ironed out as a pattern of international conformity has prevailed. The core elements of primary curricula have been summarised as:

- One or more national languages (no longer classical)
- Mathematics (universal)
- Science (introduced later than mathematics)
- Social science (history/geography/civics)
- Aesthetic education (art and music) in over 90%.

An important point to note is that these categorisations may conceal major variations in intention and practice. Local forces still have a pervasive influence on the forms and purpose of the curriculum.

An international comparative review (INCA – QCA/NFER, 1998) of curricula by the Qualifications and Curriculum Authority of England and Wales (QCA) provides the following information about the stated aims, purposes, goals and principles of 16 countries. As can be seen from Table 1.1, the elements common to all the countries cited are: *individual development* and *citizenship/community/ democracy*. It is interesting to speculate on why these are universally seen as important in preference to other, possibly more key areas, such as *knowledge/skills/understanding*.

Le Métais (1999a), the author of the INCA review from which Table 1.1 is taken, reminds us that aims, like values, reflect a country's historical context. They may also be modified in response to such imper-

Table 1.1 National educational aims (educational aims, purposes, goals and principles as stated in the documents consulted)

	England	Australia	Canada	France	Germany	Hungary	Italy	Japan	Korea	The Netherlands	New Zealand	Singapore	Spain	Sweden	Switzerland	USA
Excellence	✓	✓	✓								✓	✓			✓	✓
Individual development	✓	✓	✓	✓	✓		✓	✓	✓	✓	✓	✓			✓	✓
Social development	✓	✓	✓			✓	✓	✓	✓	✓	✓	✓	✓	✓	✓	✓
Personal qualities	✓	✓	✓				✓	✓	✓	✓	✓	✓	✓	✓		
Equal opportunity	✓	✓	✓	✓	✓	✓	✓	✓	✓	✓	✓	✓	✓	✓	✓	✓
National economy	✓	✓	✓			✓	✓	✓	✓	✓	✓	✓	✓	✓	✓	✓
Preparation for work	✓	✓	✓	✓	✓		✓	✓	✓	✓	✓	✓	✓	✓	✓	✓
Basic skills	✓	✓	✓	✓	✓		✓	✓	✓	✓	✓	✓	✓		✓	✓
Foundation for further education	✓	✓	✓	✓	✓		✓	✓	✓	✓	✓	✓	✓	✓	✓	✓
Knowledge/skills/understanding	✓	✓	✓	✓	✓		✓	✓	✓	✓	✓	✓	✓	✓	✓	✓
Citizenship/community/democracy	✓	✓	✓	✓	✓	✓	✓	✓	✓	✓	✓	✓	✓	✓	✓	
Cultural heritage/literacy		✓	✓				✓	✓	✓	✓		✓	✓	✓		
Creativity		✓	✓				✓	✓	✓	✓	✓	✓				✓
Environment		✓	✓				✓	✓	✓			✓				
Health/physical/leisure	✓	✓	✓				✓	✓	✓	✓	✓	✓	✓	✓	✓	✓
Life-long education		✓	✓				✓				✓	✓		✓		
Parental participation		✓	✓				✓				✓	✓	✓	✓	✓	
	Eng	Aust	Can	Fran	Germ	Hung	Italy	Japan	Korea	Neth	NZ	Sing	Spain	Swed	Switz	USA

Note: USA: Although education is the responsibility of individual states, the US Congress has enacted legislation, including the Goals 2000: Educate America Act.

Source: INCA (QCA/NFER, 1998).

atives as international league tables. She points out that the profession of similar values and aims does not imply similar curricular models; indeed, they can lead to the adoption of different models from country to country. In relation to this, Le Métais examines four dimensions of the values underlying different models of curricular provision (Figure 1.2.) As part of her discussion, Le Métais (1997) considers how broader values (dimension 2) are carried through into the curriculum, and she provides the following examples:

- The active promotion of multicultural knowledge, skills and understanding for all (as found in Australia, The Netherlands) or actively confronting xenophobia and intolerance (as in Sweden)

- Parity of provision by supporting religious schools (many countries) or catering for specific groups (eg Maori-medium schools in New Zealand)

- Support for minority groups to run mother-tongue classes (several countries)

- Compensatory programmes for those disadvantaged in terms of the national culture or language (most countries)

- The reassertion of national identity following political upheavals (Germany, Hungary)

- Promoting awareness of the national identity within a wider international framework (Hungary, Japan, Korea and New Zealand)

- Social cohesion (as promoted in Singapore)

1 *Centralised/decentralised* This dimension deals with individual and group freedoms to impart values and educational philosophy and/or to reflect regional or local differences through education	2 *Flexibility/stability* The degree of centralisation affects the extent to which curricula enjoy stability and/or flexibility to meet changing needs and circumstances
3 *Fostering desired attitudes through the curriculum* Broader values (including freedom, respect for the individual, social cohesion through diversity and the preservation of cultural heritage) are explicitly taught or fostered through other subjects, institutional organisation and teaching styles	4 *Values, aims and assessment* There are wide variations in the extent to which learners are assessed during the compulsory education phase and in the nature of these assessments

Figure 1.2 Le Métais' four dimensions of underlying values

So far we have considered curriculum from a national and international perspective, looking at the influences and values that underpin its construction. Although there are discernible similarities across countries in terms of stated aims and values, how these are interpreted will vary from country to country and from region to region. This is particularly true of those countries that operate a federal structure, such as the USA, Australia and Canada. In the USA, for example, responsibility for education is devolved to states and districts and the imposition of a national set of values would be seen as a threat to individual and state liberties. This strongly held 'freedom' may be illustrated by the recent decision of one state to include the Bible's version of creation in its science curriculum, in preference to more conventional evolutionary theories. In the next section we will look at how the school curriculum relates to national curriculum and international influences on learning and teaching.

⊙ *Reading*

Before moving on to the next section, please take a little time to read Jacky Lumby's chapter 'Framing learning and teaching in the 21st century', Chapter 1 of Middlewood, D. and Burton, N. (2001) *Managing the Curriculum*.

Pay particular attention to what she has to say about the emergence of individual learning as the dominant paradigm.

❏ **Our comments**

Terminology can be confusing where no shared meaning exists. 'Managing the curriculum' may refer to the implementation of national initiatives or focus on the facilitation of learning. In its widest sense, it can become equivalent to managing the whole institution. 'Managing learning and teaching' is becoming the preferred term in most western societies because it focuses on what is regarded as the core purpose of schools and colleges.

This emphasis on the individuality of the learner requires a new contract between teacher and learner and a shift in how schools and colleges manage the process of learning and teaching to encompass both individual student needs and the wider cultural needs of the communities they serve. This is clearly reflected in the INCA survey (QCA/NFER, 1998), where all the countries studied stated individual development and citizenship/community/democracy as equally important educational aims. You may wish to consider whether a tension exists between individual and communal needs and how this is addressed in your own society and institution.

The next section will start to consider some of the wider issues raised in Lumby's chapter about how the curriculum is framed to support learning and teaching.

Framing the curriculum for learning and teaching

So far we have looked at how *curriculum* may be defined and some of the common components of the curriculum across the world and over time. The content of the *curriculum* and, to some extent, the pedagogy employed in schools and colleges, may be seen as a reflection of the society within which the institution is based. Dimmock (1998), in his study of the restructuring of Hong Kong's schools, identifies the need for a 'cultural fit' between policy imperatives and the beliefs, values and behaviours of the implementers of any imported initiative. Jennings (1993, p. 141), referring to curriculum change in Caribbean schools, makes a similar point when she says:

> The need to guard against importing wholesale from developed countries any model which assumes beliefs and practices which are alien to the more impoverished developing countries has been underscored, as well as the necessity for curriculum materials to be developed which can be adapted by teachers to suit varied educational situations.

Although some universal elements, such as the teaching of mathematics, have been identified, different societies will espouse different aims for the wider curriculum, which will be reflected in its content and organisation. There has also been a discernible global trend towards centralisation of the curriculum over recent years, although this is neither a new concept nor, necessarily, significant in terms of local content or delivery. In this section we will look at the nature of the curriculum framework in order to gain an understanding of how learning and teaching may be supported and enhanced.

Some key concepts

The curriculum management challenge is to ensure the core purposes of schools and colleges are about finding optimum ways to organise learning and teaching rather than subordinating the needs of learners to the rather more easily satisfied demands of administrative convenience. The following activity is an opportunity for you to identify where you stand on some of the key issues. Go through the following sets of statements and highlight *one* definition in each set that most accurately represents your present view. If *none* of the statements corresponds to your personal belief, formulate an alternative definition.

Education is:

1. Learning how to learn.
2. Induction into a defined body of knowledge and understanding.
3. The science, art and technology of the transmission of useful knowledge.
4. The process whereby young people are given the means to acquire knowledge and understanding for themselves.
5. Or . . .

Curriculum is:

1. The school.
2. The whole body of knowledge, ideas, skills, attitudes and experiences conveyed by a school to its pupils, intentionally or otherwise.
3. The activities the organisation undertakes to achieve its goals.
4. The contrived activity and experience – organised, focused, systematic – that life, unaided, would not provide.
5. Or . . .

Management is:

1. The art and science of getting things done through other people.
2. The leadership and co-ordination of shared work.
3. Management activities, such as tasks, decision-making, developing people, setting priorities.
4. Making theories visible, practical and applying them.
5. Or . . .

❏ Our comments

First, it would be surprising if you have found this an easy exercise. It is unlikely you will have found a definition that exactly reflects your own views on curriculum, management and education. You may have found yourself both hesitating and amending the statements offered in order to produce one coherent definition.

Secondly, in reviewing your responses to, and thoughts about, these three sets of definitions, you may find it helpful to make a distinction between *inclusive* and *exclusive* statements. For example, 'Learning how to learn' is a highly inclusive statement that is very different from statement three, 'The science, art and technology of the transmission of useful knowledge', which attempts to limit what can be expected from education. Clearly, there are strengths and weaknesses in all these approaches; what is critically important is that *you* know where *you* stand.

In the Chair's conclusions at the OECD/CERI conference on 'Schooling for tomorrow' (Rotterdam, November 2000), point 10 is worth noting:

> 10. **From teaching to learning:** the curriculum is at the heart of schooling. The focus needs to shift from teaching and towards learning. Guiding the shift in focus should be the underlying aim that schools are laying the foundations for lifelong learning – the knowledge, competencies and motivation to go on learning in the many settings beyond school . . .

Lifelong learning

The statement quoted above clearly emphasises the central role of the learner in the business of schools and colleges and also highlights the enduring nature of education throughout life. The school is seen as the starting point of a process that will continue well into the future. As Lumby (2001a) notes, the World Wide Web offers global knowledge to all those with access. The emphasis in schools is therefore changing to produce people who can manipulate knowledge, understand when it has been manipulated and continue to learn and adapt, long after leaving formal education. Thus, formal education is becoming part of a wider learning context. Adult learning (like *inclusion*) is increasingly being seen as a means of developing aspects of social policy, as well as benefiting individuals. For example, the Presidency conclusions of the Lisbon Summit of the European Council (March 2000) state that 'lifelong learning is an essential policy for the development of citizenship, social cohesion and employment'. A brief look at a selection of vision statements linked to life-long learning illustrates this point:

> Lifelong learning is defined as all purposeful learning activities whether formal, non-formal or informal. A knowledge society should provide rich opportunities for learning in different contexts which are independent of where one is in the lifespan – it is not bound by age restrictions. Lifelong learning has to be based on an analysis of people's total access to knowledge and learning, within the whole range of different contexts – formal learning at school and at the university, non-formal learning in the evening class, in the residential college, at the workplace, informal learning through literature or TV and life experiences.

> Lifelong learning not only contributes to economic development, full employment and the modernising of the labour market, it also enables individuals and groups to participate in democratic, civil and cultural life, to combat racism and xenophobia, to enjoy diversity and to build social cohesion (European Association for the Education of Adults, 2001, p. 2).

> ● ALA members share a commitment to build a learning society. We believe that learning through life provides a means by which people can grow and develop, and make a contribution to the development and transformation of their own community and the society in which they live.

> ● ALA recognises the key role adult learning plays in combating poverty, inequality, ignorance and social exclusion as well as promoting democracy, creativity, imagination and economic development (Adult Learning Australia, 2001).

The AAACE is dedicated to the belief that lifelong learning contributes to human fulfilment and positive social change. We envision a more humane world made possible by the diverse practice of our members in helping adults acquire the knowledge, skills, and values needed to lead productive and satisfying lives (American Association for Adult and Continuing Education, 2001).

Our vision of the Learning Age is about more than employment. The development of a culture of learning will help to build a united society, assist in the creation of personal independence, and encourage our creativity and innovation. Learning encompasses basic literacy to advanced scholarship. We learn in many different ways through formal study, reading, watching television, going on a training course, taking an evening class, at work, and from family and friends (DfEE, 1998, s. 2:8).

Those working in post-compulsory education will recognise a dual role here. First, they are part of the provision for life-long learning – students and trainees may wish or need to learn at any age – and, secondly, they perform a vital role in encouraging their students to 'learn how to learn' so they will feel enabled to return when more learning is needed. Thus, whilst the syllabus provided may be very focused upon a particular technical, vocational or academic area, it may also contain opportunities for students to acquire or refresh their study skills and to reflect upon what they have learned and how they have learned it.

Curriculum models

So far we have been engaged in what might be called 'ground clearing'. We have seen that the debate about the nature and purpose of education has been continuing for thousands of years, without achieving any uncontested outcomes. David Stow (cited in Lofthouse, 1992, p. 97), a pioneer of teacher training, summed up the ambivalence that still persists when he wrote (in 1836):

Till within the last few years, the term used to define Education was *instruction*. Give elementary and religious *instruction*, it was said and still is said, and this will be sufficient. Teach the poor to read the Bible, and forthwith you make them good, holy and happy citizens – kind parents, obedient children – compassionate and honourable in their dealings; and crime will diminish. Hundreds of thousands of our population have received such an education. Are such the results?

You may detect a note of exasperation in Stow's words when he (ironically) inquires whether the intended outcomes of the prescribed instruction have been achieved. Leaving aside the misplaced optimism of the prescription described by Stow, it may be helpful to look more closely at his opening statement – that education equals instruction. If this statement were true, the task of curriculum management becomes relatively easy:

- Curriculum equals timetable.
- Be instrumental in your approach.
- Sort the subjects, match the assessment schedules, deploy the staff.
- Job done!

Although Stow's comments may appear to be largely irrelevant today, the imposition of national schemes of work, such as the UK's National Literacy Strategy (in 1998), which prescribes what and how to teach, can be seen as equally limiting in terms of what is included and how it is seen as the key to redressing pupil underachievement (an implied factor in social disaffection). In colleges, vocational curricula may be prescribed by national organisations (in the UK called 'lead bodies') representing particular business, legal, manufacturing or public sector areas, which decide in fine detail what is deemed to be currently relevant in their professional or vocational area. These current and historical examples serve as illustrations of the various ways in which a curriculum may be presented.

11

For a different perspective, look at David Middlewood's 'four layer' model in Chapter 7 of Middlewood and Burton (2001, p. 109), which is used to describe the basic dimensions or stages of the curriculum:

1.   The *rhetorical* curriculum (what is stated in policies and statements of aims)

2.   The *planned* curriculum (found in schemes of work, syllabuses)

3.   The *delivered* curriculum (how it is taught in classrooms or through other media)

4.   The *received* curriculum (what is ultimately in the minds and some would say hearts of the students).

Activity

The curriculum experience

Analyse the curriculum experience for students of a lesson you have recently given or observed. Begin by noting the structure, content, activities and outcomes, rather as you would when preparing a lesson plan. Consider how each of these elements fits the pattern outlined above and to what extent there is a difference between the intended and the actual experience. If you encourage students to practise self-evaluation, you may also wish to take their comments into account.

❏ Our comments

You may have found the lesson was of an instructional nature and that consistency between the *rhetorical*, the *intended*, the *offered* and the *received* curriculum was instrumental in achieving what you set out to do. On the other hand, especially where the lesson is structured in a way that allows for student participation and feedback, the *rhetorical*, *intended*, *delivered* and *received* aspects of the curriculum may well have differed or evolved from what was planned.

You may also have noted that the received curriculum may not be the same for all individuals and groups. While student participation enriches learning, unintended inequalities may impoverish it. In a group that encompasses a wide ability range, there are likely to be important questions about accessibility. How does the notion of differentiation affect intended outcomes for all students?

In studying this 'four layer' model, you will have become more aware of something you probably knew intuitively: the difference between *rhetoric* and *reality*. In terms of managing the curriculum, there are increasing pressures on managers at all levels in schools and colleges to eliminate gaps between the intended and presented curricula.

According to Crombie White (1997), the locus of control has moved from schools to national bodies for a number of reasons, including:

* Inconsistent provision and standards across schools
* Out-of-date curricula
* Conflicting ideologies
* The emergence of a wide array of stakeholders.

Schools and teachers have responded to a perceived (and actual) threat to their professional autonomy by either 'teaching to the tests' or by resorting to the well established strategy of 'personalising' the curriculum to meet local needs. The following quotation, taken from Crombie White (1997, p. 23), sums up the worst fears of teachers everywhere:

Education has become a commodity to be bought and sold, schools and colleges have become the providers of a service to consumers, teachers have become the deliverers of a curriculum to the specification of the government, delivery is evaluated against performance indicators created by market regulators (who are not professionals) and institutions are audited to check on the mechanisms of quality control.

This rather extreme view may, or may not, mirror your own thoughts and experiences. We will examine the role of *assessment* in some detail in Chapter 3, but it is useful to note here the enormous influence that assessment, in all its aspects, has had on the curriculum and, therefore, on teaching. Bottery's (1992) model in *The Ethics of Educational Management* neatly shows how one educational philosophy (cultural transmission) leads to accountability and evaluation through assessment practices that are clear and precise, probably quantitative in nature, administered via formal examinations. Hargreaves (1984, p. 2) describes various aspects of assessing achievement, prominent amongst which are written, public examinations that require 'the capacity to retain propositional knowledge, and act from such knowledge appropriately in response to a specified request, and to do so quickly without reference to possible sources of information'. Although assessment has, in many cases, moved on from such a narrow focus, this type of examination, with minor modifications, is still typical across the world.

The prescribed curriculum

Teaching a prescribed curriculum is often associated with a lack of spontaneity and creativity so that teachers (and consequently their teaching) become outcomes focused. This, of course, is the intention and allows the prescribing body a higher degree of control and standardisation than a more autonomous curriculum model would permit.

The extent to which schools and teachers are consulted about what and how they should teach is a good indicator of how well a national curriculum will be accepted and delivered. There are significant differences in approaches to curriculum consultation and design across countries; a few examples will suffice to give you an idea of what is possible. In the UK, the National Curriculum, written by a body of subject 'specialists' appointed by the government, was introduced into schools after a four-month consultation that included an average six-week summer break, when schools were closed. In contrast, Spain put out proposals on the curriculum after pilot schemes had been evaluated, followed by three years of consultation and debate before the final version was introduced. In Greece, the curriculum is taught through a series of textbooks, which are drawn up by the Pedagogical Institute on behalf of the government. There is some consultation with schools, but the ultimate decision rests with the Ministry of National Education and Religions. The USA has no national curriculum, with 1,600 school boards serving 110,000 schools. The San Juan Unified School District in the State of California employs a school board that invites staff members and a citizens' committee to review state-approved textbooks and classroom materials and make recommendations for purchase, although the final decisions are made by the school board. Clearly defined academic standards describe what students are expected to know and be able to do at each level and in each subject. Singapore, generally regarded as a highly prescriptive and controlled society, is currently moving to allow schools more individual autonomy in creating their own identity and the emphasis will be on education for living rather than examinations, all within an ICT-driven education system (Chong and Leong, 2000).

Colleges of further education may be more comfortable with the 'market-driven' economy described by Crombie White. They have also arguably been more closely shaped on a historical basis by national forces than by internal autonomy. Their academic curricula have been influenced by the nationally shaped curricula of schools and the entry requirements and generic curriculum structures of universities. Their vocational curricula have developed in response to the needs of particular professions and workplaces, sometimes mediated at a local level by the specialist demands of local employers.

Becher (1989) describes the difference between government rhetoric and classroom reality as 'the implementation gap' and looks at how a school is likely to react to the imposition of a centralised curriculum. First, he defines three structural levels:

1. The school as a whole

2. Constituent departments

3. Individual staff members.

Within this operational arena, Becher examines the possibilities of coercive, manipulative and rational approaches to curriculum implementation within hierarchical, political or collegial schools (see Table 1.2). Acknowledging that, while all institutions will 'mix and match' the above approaches according to individual circumstances, Becher nevertheless offers important insights into how typical schools may respond to the imposition of a centrally determined curriculum.

Table 1.2 Hierarchical, political or collegial schools

The hierarchical school	The political school	The collegial school
Strong hierarchical structures	Bureaucratic organisation	Professionally
Plays safe	Pressure groups	orientated
Coercive managers	Political manipulation of	Rational approach
Emphasises test	decision-making	Pupils' best interests
scores/exam results	Power struggles	Mixed-ability teaching
Follows curriculum	Little integration or coherence	Cross-curricular
directives slavishly	'Balkanised' curriculum	Topic-based activity
Rigid subject/time boundaries	provision	Testing not overemphasised

Source: Becher (1989).

Becher's analysis is persuasive and important. Governments can make policies and issue legislation, but they cannot ensure that what is intended is delivered. The diversity of institutions, allied to the differing roles and attitudes of their curriculum implementers, means that, in reality, governments are incapable of reducing the 'implementation gap' beyond a modest degree. In this context, the role of the curriculum manager as *gatekeeper* – accepting or deflecting curriculum innovations – is an important aspect of curriculum control and implementation, which will be considered in more detail later in this chapter.

Activity

Personalising the curriculum

Make notes on the way in which a particular curriculum initiative has been altered ('personalised') by those responsible for its delivery, by considering how variations and accommodations are incorporated at different levels, from senior management down to individual classroom level. Identify the macro and micro features related to the implementation gap.

❏ **Our comments**

You will probably find an external requirement has been subverted within the closed box of the class-room or in the light of the perceived needs of individual students. Individual departments may also modify programmes of study to reflect local conditions or to fit resource imperatives. A good example of this is the notion of *differentiation* of curriculum content and delivery to take account of the special educational needs of students within a class.

The macro elements may be associated with a lack of resources or adequate training for curriculum delivery.

The micro elements may well be much more difficult to analyse but will be a reflection of the relation-ships between people and different attitudes in the school or college.

Curriculum control

The curriculum in schools and colleges has traditionally been seen as the preserve of educational pro-fessionals, although the reality of this view is open to question, both historically and geographically. A distinction needs to be drawn between what is, or has been, *required* to be taught and what is, or has been, *actually* taught. The CERI/OECD Illinois conference in 1971 considered a paper by Marklund ('Frame factors and curriculum development') in which he discussed the different roles of the politicians and the professionals in setting curriculum objectives and translating them into practice. He argued:

> School has long been regarded as a community on its own, a state within the state with its own rules. This is no longer true. School is now looked upon as forming part of the community as a whole, an open system, in which the objectives and forms of work in the community are reflected in those of the school, that is to say in curriculum development (OECD, 1973, p. 12).

The conference delegates went on to discuss the relationship between central control of the curriculum and local decision-making, agreeing that a balance needed to be achieved '. . . between central plan-ning and local control to insure [*sic*] adequate uniformity to reach society's goals while at the same time promoting sufficient variation to accommodate local needs' (OECD, 1973, p. 39). At that time, the debate was concentrated on how to involve teachers in curriculum planning, although one discus-sion group questioned whether the net effect of teacher involvement might be to 'dilute the intellectual component which is the major strength of curriculum developments undertaken by experts outside of school systems' (ibid., p. 40).

School teachers and college lecturers have always been subject to external constraints on *what* they teach and the conditions in which they operate will, to a large extent, dictate *how* they will teach. Control may, of course, be seen as benign: promoting equality and coherence, or coercive: imposing prescriptive, 'one size fits all' programmes.

The selection of what is an appropriate and relevant curriculum may be undertaken at several differ-ent levels. Lawton (1983) and Becher and Kogan (1992) identify five levels of control in the educational system. These are as follows:

1. *National* Central government, ministers and civil servants, technical and professional 'standard keepers', national pressure groups and quasi-government agencies.

2. *Local* Local government, including elected representatives, officers and advisers, local employers, pressure groups, religious groups, local agencies.

3. *Institutional* Schools and colleges, including governing bodies, principals, teachers and students, pressure groups of parents, employers and the local community.

4. *Departmental* Faculties, departments or other subunits that have a functional responsibility for a specific subject or other defined element of the curriculum. These include heads of department, subject co-ordinators, specialist staff and subject-specific pressure groups.

5. *Individual* Teachers or lecturers in their classrooms, laboratories or workshops. They have a defined responsibility for delivering a specific aspect of the curriculum to a class or group. They may be subject to pressure from parents, employers and others concerned about the impact on particular students.

Groups and individuals at various levels may be able to deflect pressure from superordinate levels, as we noted earlier ('personalising' the curriculum). This tendency of schools and colleges to modify national imperatives, by selecting what they perceive as relevant, may deflect, explicitly or implicitly, those curricular innovations they do not support or 'own'.

Activity

Levels of control and curriculum aspects

The matrix shown in Figure 1.3 links the five levels of decision-making to six conceptually discrete aspects of curriculum control. This two-part activity is designed to encourage you to think about the relative importance of each of the five levels in respect of the six aspects of curriculum and to assess the significance of *lay* and *professional* interests at each level:

1. In relation to each of the six aspects, rank the five levels according to their relative importance in influencing or determining that aspect of the curriculum ('1' = most important, '5' = least important). There should be a number in each cell.
2. For each of the 30 cells, please indicate whether the main influence is professional ('P') or lay ('L').

Aspect	1 Aims	2 Content	3 Pedagogy	4 Evaluation	5 Resources	6 Assessment
Level 1 National						
Level 2 Local						
Level 3 Insitutional						
Level 4 Departmental						
Level 5 Individual						

Figure 1.3 Relationship between levels of control and curriculum aspects
Source: Adapted from Lawton (1983, p. 120)

This is a long and complex activity that will require some time and thought to complete. However, it goes to the heart of curriculum control and should help you reflect on these important issues in relation to your own understanding and professional practice.

❑ Our comments

Your responses are likely to be influenced by a number of factors:

- The national and local educational system in which you are working.
- The phase of education in which you are particularly interested: primary, secondary, further, special education, etc.
- The position you hold within the system.

The balance between lay and professional involvement varies markedly according to the level and aspect under consideration. National policies may have been strongly influenced by political interests but professionals remain significant in local delivery. Within the school, teachers remain central to most curriculum decisions because lay governors are generally reluctant to intervene in what they regard as professional matters, although they may have a legal obligation to ensure overall curriculum requirements are met.

The delivery of the curriculum remains the responsibility of individual teachers in their classrooms. High-quality learning and teaching depend primarily on the quality and motivation of these teachers, irrespective of the national framework within which they operate.

The role of the state

Before moving on to look at the role of stakeholders in influencing the curriculum at the various levels described above, it will be useful to consider some important issues relating to the influences and control operating at the national level. The role of the state in defining the curriculum can be a complicated knot to unravel; on the one hand, as we have already noted, education systems are seen as a legitimate way of ensuring the culture and beliefs of society are passed on to future generations. However, this perfectly understandable aspiration can be perverted to serve the requirements of totalitarian states such as happened in Nazi Germany, the former Soviet Union or South Africa under the system of apartheid. Coulby (2000) discusses the breakdown of the Soviet Union in this connection, looking at the aftermath in eastern Europe as the newly re-formed states rediscover their national identity after a period during which they became what he calls 'the victims of state knowledge'. Under the rule of Moscow, teaching at every level of the system was partial, if not prejudiced, in favour of the Soviet ideal and the pre-eminence of Russia. In this sense, therefore, there was a distinct variance between education and society. Coulby contrasts the transitions to be seen in the emerging states of eastern Europe with the transitions that are occurring in western Europe and the USA as follows:

Eastern Europe

- Political freedom.
- Economic liberalisation.
- Nationalism.
- Breakdown of social order.
- Renewed interest in the West.

The USA and Western Europe

- Reconfiguration of global capitalism.
- Uncontested US political power.
- Rapid development of ICT and the related emergence of the knowledge economy.
- 'Postmodernism.'
- Revised interest in the East.

Education systems have been adapted to address the changing circumstances of the eastern bloc nations and the role of schools and universities in this transformation is currently the subject of negotiation. Coulby identifies a number of key issues that are relevant to this process:

- With the re-emergence of a national identity, language teaching now occupies a central place in the curriculum. The language of instruction in some states, such as Estonia, Latvia and Lithuania, is no longer Russian and the first foreign language also need no longer be Russian.
- Marxist-Leninism has been abandoned as the paradigm discourse for a variety of subjects.
- History has been rewritten to reflect the national, rather than the Soviet, perspective.
- The centralism of the national culture has led to a change of emphasis across subjects or new subjects being introduced, such as folk song and folk dance in Latvia.

There is, of course, a thin line between nation-building and nationalism and, as Coulby (2000, pp. 8–9) points out:

> . . . the re-writing of history and the celebration of culture too readily focused on a narrow definition of what the nation was, who the true citizens were, and who the historical enemies had been. The rediscovery of the nation and the national identity was accompanied by a rediscovery or recreation of the other.

He goes on to claim that, in this reassertion of nationalism, the schools and universities 'played their parts', illustrating this by noting that a 'surprising number' of university academics were not only fervent Serbian nationalists but also became the architects of so called ethnic cleansing. Coulby poses a number of important questions, two of which have a clear relationship to the curriculum debate in which we are engaged:

1. To what extent are school, college and university curricula legitimate policy implements for the task of nation-building?

2. Do major political and economic changes necessitate changes in education systems?

In reflecting upon these questions, you may wish to draw parallels between what we understand to be happening in Eastern Europe and examples closer to your own experience. In the UK, for instance, the recent devolution of power to the Scottish Parliament and the Welsh Assembly, along with the removal of direct rule from Northern Ireland, have resulted in a reconfiguration of each national education system. The case of Wales is a perfect example of the way national identity is seen to be consolidated through its language, with the confirmation of Welsh as the required medium of instruction in the less anglicised parts of Wales, despite a large, English-speaking population.

The role of stakeholders

In the previous section we identified five levels of influence on the curriculum as the starting point for our discussion of social control. We also noted the growing importance of the global perspective and, implicit in all our discussions, is the part the students, themselves, play, both as recipients and influencers of the curriculum (see Margaret Preedy's comments on students as stakeholders in Chapter 6 of Middlewood and Burton, 2001, pp. 98–101). If we attempt to represent these layers in diagrammatic form, the model may look something like a nest of boxes, with the most influential players, or stakeholders, nearest the centre. The placing of the different interest groups is open to debate, according to the factors at play in a particular cultural, social and political situation. As a starting point, Figure 1.4 shows what might be considered as the standard model for the UK.

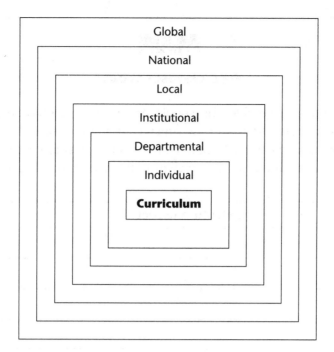

Figure 1.4 Influences on the curriculum

Using the examples given in the previous section for the five levels of control (Lawton, 1983; Becher and Kogan, 1992) you will be able to identify the stakeholders at each level and relate these to your own context. At the global level, we would include political and economic affiliations and the Internet; you may be able to identify more. A useful illustration of how many stakeholders may be exerting an influence on the curriculum is to be found in Burton *et al.* (2001, p. 30, Figure 2.4). This identifies no fewer than 15 major players in relation to curriculum design in further education in the UK.

The influences at work both within and outside the institution will have an effect on many aspects of what goes on in schools and colleges, not only in terms of content and delivery of the curriculum but in how the school or college organises its management structures. This may be implicit: in a one-teacher school, for example, the management structure is, of necessity, simple. In larger organisations, the management structure is more complex but its nature is, to a large extent, dictated by external influences, such as the availability of funding for posts of responsibility, 'tagged' funding or inspection regimes that assume particular configurations of management and organisation. In Chapter 3 we will examine curriculum management in greater detail but it will be useful to keep in mind how your own institution organises this aspect as we consider the potential contribution of a wide variety of stakeholders to curriculum determination.

In deciding what is to be taught, all stakeholders, at whatever level of influence, are confronted by choice. There is a vast array of human knowledge from which to choose and what is *not* selected will, inevitably, be greater than what is. Not all the available knowledge will be true or accurate and the choice of 'false' knowledge can be deliberate (remember the rewriting of history) or unavoidable (due to our own state of understanding at any one time – the earth is not, after all, flat). We need to adopt some sort of criteria for selection – what Coulby (2000) refers to as 'knowledge protocols'. Each group of stakeholders will devise its own criteria for selecting one item in preference to another but the real question is who should be allowed to choose? The following activity asks you to make some choices yourself.

Activity

Who chooses what?

Listed below is a selection of stakeholders in schools and colleges. You may wish to add more in the spaces provided. For each group, try to identify which aspect of the curriculum you feel they should be given responsibility for, in choosing its main components. You could exclude some groups if you feel they do not have a legitimate voice. You may also decide to rank them in order of importance.

Stakeholder group	Curriculum aspect
Students	
Academics	
Philosophers	
Teachers	
Employers	
Governors	
Parents	
Inspectors	
Politicians	
Religious authorities	
Local authorities	

❑ Our comments

Everyone feels he or she has a stake in education and his or her views on what should be taught in schools and colleges will be based on his or her own experience and understanding. Each stakeholder group will consider they have a valuable perspective that gives them the right to select, if not specific content, then some of the overall aims for the curriculum. Teachers, for example, from their position at the cutting edge of education, will feel they have a legitimate claim to decide what is appropriate for the students they teach and how it should be taught. Philosophers will consider the whole domain of human knowledge and the ways in which humanity has used this knowledge to articulate their proposals. Politicians will be influenced by the views formed whilst working in their original professions, as well as seeing education as the key to achieving national and cultural aims. As 'consumers', students will be keen to access a curriculum that not only engages their interest and enthusiasm but is also demonstrably relevant in the here and now and will be of future value.

It is harder to rank stakeholders' claims to influence in order of importance unless there is a clear idea of what we mean by 'important'. Your definition will reflect your own perspective and vested interest and may be based on the 'ideal' or the reality of your own situation. *Importance* may be an ethical judgement or a recognition of who holds the power.

Everard and Morris (1996, p. 177) identify eight main questions to which stakeholders should be invited to respond. These are reproduced below:

(1) What are our aims and values as a school or college?

(2) In what order of priority do we rank our aims?

(3) What economic, technical and social changes do we anticipate over the coming years?

(4) What are the implications for the lives of the children in our schools [or the learners in our colleges]? What are the threats and what are the opportunities? (The mark of a healthy organization or individual is a focus on the opportunities in change rather than the threats.)

(5) How do we need to adapt the curriculum?

(6) Given the needs we have identified, how do our resources match these? What are the strengths and weaknesses of our resources?

(7) How do we need to develop or adapt our resources?

(8) What should be our action plan?

Institutional values, culture and ethos

In the previous section we began to identify the impact of various stakeholders on schools and colleges and how their influence has a bearing on what is taught. Schools and colleges respond to these internal and external pressures in different ways to create their own institutional values, culture and ethos. This differentiated response is what makes each school or college unique within local or national systems of education and provides necessary choice and diversity for both teachers and learners. Whilst there are clearly universal values that are claimed by all schools and colleges, such as ensuring an entitlement for students to a broad, balanced and relevant curriculum (Dimmock, 2000), there will, inevitably, be other values that may be articulated only by certain sectors or institutions. An example of this may be the core values expressed by a school with a particular religious affiliation, such as the general aims of the Islamic Institutes of the Diwan of the Royal Court, Sultanate of Oman, as reproduced below:

1. To appreciate the aesthetic value and contemplation on God-creation, in order to develop the students' awareness in the frame of the Islamic thoughts.

2. To develop the learner's humanity and develop the feeling of his/her citizenship and nationality.

3. To develop artistic awareness through contemplation and appreciation of aesthetic value of God-creation, nature and understand Omani heritage.

4. To develop loyalty to Oman as the mother country, Islamic brotherhood nations and the other worldwide friendly countries.

5. To prepare scholars who can hold the responsibility of guiding others to the right direction of the religious life.

6. To prepare well qualified Imams [the person who leads prayers in mosques] who can successfully hold such important posts.

7. To prepare Shariat [Islamic law] judges.

8. To understand Omani, Arabic and Islamic artistic heritage (Al Tobi, 2001).

The core values of the institution need to be shared by teachers, students, parents and other stakeholders (to an equal or lesser degree) if they are to support the learning aims at the heart of the organisation. In order to promote this necessary sharing of values, they must be understood and agreed by the key players, as well as being clearly articulated for the benefit of external bodies who may exercise a monitoring or inspectorial function. The values upheld by a school or college are commonly expressed as aims or mission statements. The following examples are drawn from a selection of schools and colleges in England; you may wish to compare them with your own institution's published aims:

This school offers free, high quality education to students from 11–19. Working in partnership with students, parents, industry and the community, the staff seeks to enable and empower students to set and review their own targets for growth and reach them with maturity (technology college).

God is at the heart of this school. We provide a Catholic education for all, through a curriculum which caters for the needs of each child. Each of us is special and unique. We support and guide each other in our Christian journeys of faith. We work together to provide appropriate opportunities which will enable children to achieve their full potential in everything they do (Roman Catholic primary school).

We want what you want – the best possible education for your child. Our aim is to offer every pupil the right amount of **challenge** in a **supportive** environment to ensure maximum achievement (secondary comprehensive school).

This College is a force for change which will promote and support energetically economic employment and individual development for the actual and potential workforce, locally and regionally. The pursuit of Quality, Equality and Value will inform all that we do.

Our approach to delivering this mission for the next five years is to become more than a college by offering more than a qualification (further education college).

The mission of this college is to make a significantly beneficial and lasting contribution to the lifelong learning of the people of this city and county aged 16 and over. For every one of its students and employees the college is committed to maintaining the highest standards in every sphere of its activity, and to providing the widest opportunities for achievement and personal development (sixth form college).

To strive to provide the best education, in a secure Islamic environment, through the knowledge and application of the Qur'an & Sunnah (Islamic primary school).

We believe that school should provide a stimulating working environment that is happy, secure and organised for the academic, physical, aesthetic, emotional and moral development of the children, an atmosphere in which learning skills can be acquired. We aim to encourage children to be self-motivated, self-disciplined and self-reliant as far as possible (junior school).

This school believes it should work to create an ethos where all pupils are valued equally. Within this understanding, it aims to provide opportunities for intellectual, personal and social development in order that pupils may realise their potential. Learning should be exciting and relevant, encouraging pupils to become purposeful members of school, the community and society (special school).

To provide education and training to enable people to achieve their full potential in work and society (land-based college).

The examples quoted above reflect what these schools and colleges perceive to be important or right for them. In any list of aims, priorities will need to be set, according to what is felt to be most important *at that time*. Thus the values of an organisation will change over time, in response to both the internal and external pressures that may be operating. Institutional priorities arise out of a number of individual priorities that make up the value system of the organisation. Everard and Morris (1996), writing in the context of schools, believe it is the task of the headteacher or principal, with the help of the staff curriculum group, to take account of the existing value system when putting together:

- The aims, values and priorities of the school
- The curriculum towards which the school will move
- The rationale behind these.

In further education colleges, both the college aims and the curriculum to which it aspires may be strongly focused on local and national priorities; this does not prevent the college from having its own values and purpose, within which those aims and curriculum activities are carried out. For example, see the comment from a further education college above where the aspirations are 'to become more than a college by offering more than a qualification'.

Atkin (1999) identifies a number of concepts that emerge most frequently when groups of educators are asked to identify the core values fundamental to their educative purpose. These are:

- Self-worth/self-actualisation
- Knowledge/insight
- Responsibility
- Creativity
- Trust
- Achievement/success
- Growth
- Confidence/competence
- Integration/wholeness
- Rights/respect
- Equity
- Adaptability.

She sees a tension between a political driving force focused on outcomes that serve the economic system and the educative driving force that is focused on developing the understandings, skills and attributes that make us more fully human. The values and beliefs of a school or college are linked to its principles and practices and this relationship is illustrated in the model given in Figure 1.5.

Many schools and colleges would be able to claim they have identified and articulated their core values and beliefs and that these are firmly encapsulated within their mission statement and/or policy statements. However, the translation of these into practice, what Atkin terms the 'living expression of your values', is often where difficulties may arise. Sullivan (2000, p. 5) suggests an activity that helps us to identify our *enacted* values as opposed to our *espoused* values.

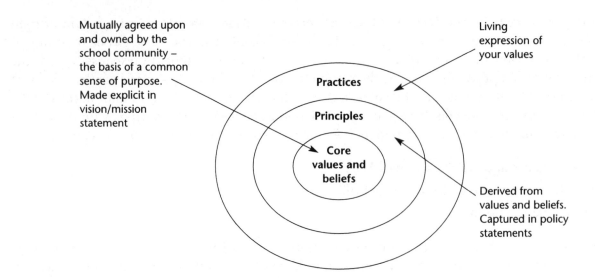

Figure 1.5 The relationship between core values, beliefs and practices
Source: Atkin (1996)

Activity

Identifying the values in practice

In this activity we ask you to start with one of your school's or college's practices and to work backwards to identify the values that are embedded within it. The practice we would like you to consider is how your institution recognises achievement. The questions you will need to ask are:

- Is achievement recognised?
- Whose achievement is recognised?
- How is achievement recognised?
- How often is achievement recognised?

❏ Our comments

Sullivan (2000) asks: were the examples you found related only to student achievement? What does this say about teachers and how their work is valued? Do only individuals receive recognition of achievement, or do teams, classes or departments receive recognition of their collective achievements? Is competition valued, or co-operation? Is sporting prowess more important than academic achievement, and where do social and civic achievements fit in? She makes the point that these reflections on your practice are, in fact, ethical questions and goes on to say (ibid., p. 6) that:

> Often we fail to recognise the ethical dimension of everyday events such as: giving detentions or suspending or excluding a student; bullying and how teachers and school leaders react to reports of or witnessing this; deciding whether students can participate in decisions which affect them at school; or practices adopted with 'at risk' students.

In identifying the practices relating to recognising achievement, how easy was it to match these practices to the stated aims or policies of your school or college? If you found an 'implementation gap' (Becher, 1989) between policy and practice, this would not be unusual. The reasons for this may be more difficult to unpick and may be related to communication problems within the institution or lack of 'ownership' or understanding of policies and how these relate to agreed aims.

Institutional culture and the hidden curriculum

So far we have looked at the values and beliefs that underpin the work of educational institutions and that have an impact on both the content of the curriculum and on the way the curriculum is delivered. These values and beliefs and the practices or behaviour that are linked to these form the basis of what we refer to as the *culture* or *ethos* of the institution. Torrington and Weightman (1993) argue that these two terms may be used to describe aspects of the same thing, commenting that 'culture' is more common in management circles and 'ethos' is more often used in education circles, particularly when referring to the children in a school. Cultural norms are developed over time, based on the core values held by the school or college. The stronger the core set of values, the stronger will be the culture. Sergiovanni (1989) sees the values, beliefs and norms as more important than the structure of the school itself, since the structure rests upon the foundations these provide. An understanding of the culture within a school or a college will assist in both facilitating and effecting change, as well as allowing a deeper appreciation of how the institution defines its curricular aims and promotes learning and teaching:

> Culture is often not expressed and may be known without being understood. It is nonetheless real and powerful, so that the enthusiasts who unwittingly work counter-culturally will find that there is a metaphorical but solid brick wall against which they are beating their heads. Enthusiasts who pause to work out the nature of their school culture can at least begin the process of change and influence the direction of the cultural evolution, because culture can never be like a brick wall. It is living, growing and vital, able to strengthen and support the efforts of those who use it, as surely as it will frustrate the efforts of those who ignore it (Torrington and Weightman, 1993, p. 46).

The culture of a school gives rise to what is commonly referred to as the 'hidden' curriculum: that which is absorbed by students at almost an unconscious level. The structures, practices and norms of an organisation have to be learnt in order to function within that particular context, yet are rarely clearly articulated; the students (and staff) pick up what is required by observing others and drawing inferences from what is said and done. The hidden curriculum may, or may not, reflect the stated aims and values of the school or college. In the area of equal opportunities, for example, practice may well trail behind policy, with the result that even quite young children will quickly learn that equality of opportunity does not, necessarily, mean equality of access, especially if you happen to be a quiet girl in a classroom full of noisy, attention-seeking boys!

Figure 1.6 provides a model or framework that may help you start to analyse the culture in your own school or college. Start by referring to the *conceptual intangible foundations* (small inner circle) – the values, philosophy and ideology of the institution – and see how they can be related to the tangible expressions and symbolism (the 18 manifestations to be found in the large oval). You will need to identify how all these internal elements link with the external community in order to develop a fuller understanding of all the factors at play. This type of detailed cultural analysis is both interesting and useful. In addition to providing a deeper understanding of what the school stands for and 'the way we do things around here' (Deal, 1985), the culture of the school or college needs to be understood because a mismatch of action and culture can produce ineffective action (Torrington and Weightman, 1993). Cultural analysis also serves a number of important management purposes:

1. It offers an indicator of the match between internal organisation and external environmental values.

2. It leads to a more complete understanding of how things are done in a particular institution.

3. It facilitates assessment of which areas of individual and organisational activity are in conflict with the desired organisational culture.

4. It suggests areas of activity that may be open to influence in order to promote desired organisational values (based on Bush and West-Burnham, 1994).

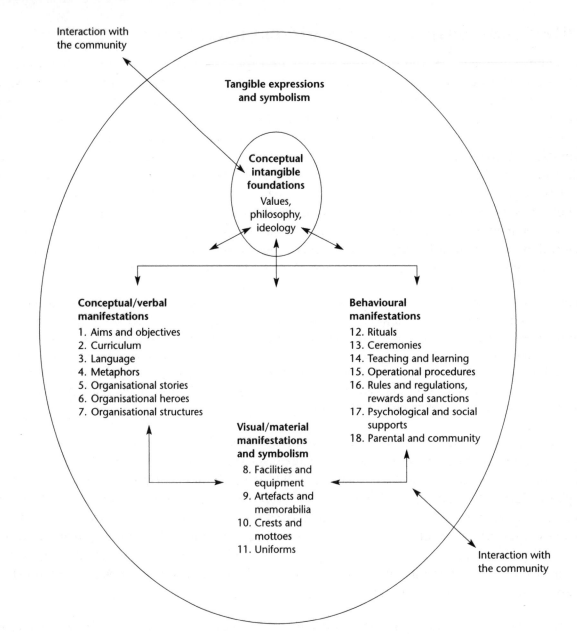

Figure 1.6 A framework for describing and analysing the culture of a school
Source: Beare *et al.* (1989, p. 176)

The 'primary mechanisms' of cultural change and consolidation have been described by Schein (1985) as:

1. What leaders pay most attention to

2. How leaders react to crises and critical incidents

3. Role modelling, teaching and coaching by leaders

4. Criteria for allocating rewards and determining status

5. Criteria for selection, promotion and termination.

Following on from the primary mechanisms listed above, Schein also describes 'secondary mechanisms' for the articulation and reinforcement of culture. These are:

1. The organisational structure

2. Systems and procedures

3. Spaces, buildings and façades

4. Stories and legends about important events and people

5. Formal statements of philosophy and policy.

A couple of points worth noting here are that cultural leaders are not, necessarily, the same as hierarchical leaders and that there may be a collection of subcultures (teacher vs. student culture, for example) within an overarching school culture. In a large college there may be subcultures of departments or college sites that have more influence on the day-to-day experience of students and teachers than the overarching college culture. If these differences are an expression of the variety that exists in any organisation, but are firmly based on the collective values and beliefs of that organisation, then there is little to worry about. If, however, these differences are indications of a lack of coherence or agreement about core values or beliefs, the cultural integrity of the school or college is threatened.

We have been using the term *culture* in a very specific way to mean the educational ethos of the school or college, based on its expressed values, beliefs and reflected in its actions and behaviour. It is important to remember, however, that the common meaning of culture, as related to national identity, also has an impact on the internal culture of many educational institutions in a pluralistic society. Schools and colleges that serve a wide variety of ethnic groups will be at pains to find a set of core values that gain agreement across a wide range of social and religious beliefs, whilst reflecting the 'host' culture sufficiently to meet local and national requirements.

Issues of equity

It is unlikely any educational institution or government ministry would fail to include some statement about equity in its overall aims for education. As reported by Atkin (1999), one of the core values consistently expressed by educators is that of equity and a review of school and college prospectuses will generally yield some statement about equal opportunities or student entitlement. These statements will, of course, differ in their emphasis or degree of sophistication, depending on the cultural context (societal and institutional). The Queensland (Australia) School Curriculum Council publishes a detailed framework for promoting equity in its schools. The following extract from their website (August 2001) gives an indication of its scope:

> The Queensland School Curriculum Council is committed to ensuring that principles of equity underpin curriculum and test development. Syllabuses and associated curriculum materials are designed to support an education that enables all students to reach their potential, and to contribute effectively to building a fairer, more harmonious future. [. . .] An equitable curriculum acknowledges that power in any society is not equally shared; that contemporary power relations are shaped historically, culturally and socially; and that they are reflected in the operations of major social institutions, including schools. The Council is committed to developing inclusive curriculum [*sic*] in which:
>
> - Students' learning encompasses the experiences, knowledge, values and perspectives of the least advantaged, as well as the most advantaged groups in society
>
> - Students develop an understanding of, and respect for, diversity within and between social groups
>
> - Students develop the knowledge, skills, attitudes and agency to question and challenge inequality and injustice.

Equity is a difficult concept to define and is often used interchangeably with the term *equal*. Although the two words are related, they do not mean the same thing, as a simple comparison of dictionary definitions will show:

Equal   *the same in quantity, quality, size, degree, rank, level, etc.*

Equity   *fairness; the application of general principles of justice to correct or supplement the law* (*Concise Oxford Dictionary*, 1995).

Thus it is not accurate to say that equity requires we treat all students the same; this would clearly be unfair and disadvantage some students who, for various reasons, could not gain full advantage from what was on offer. The promotion of equity demands we make reasonable and appropriate accommodations to promote access and attainment for all students. An obvious illustration of this process is the way students with special needs are enabled to access the curriculum (see Sommefeldt's discussion of individual school responses in Chapter 10 of Middlewood and Burton, 2001).

The key areas relating to equity in schools and colleges can be categorised as follows:

1. Gender (*male/female, sexual orientation*).

2. Socioeconomic status (*wealth/poverty, unskilled/professional*).

3. Ethnicity (*host culture/minority ethnic groups*).

4. Special needs (*ability/disability*).

5. Location (*urban/rural, inner city/suburban*).

6. Type of school (*high/low achievement, well resourced/poor facilities*).

Although it is not always possible for schools and colleges fully to compensate for such factors as poverty or the lack of civic facilities commonly associated with rural areas, an awareness of the implications of each of these categories on the design and delivery of the curriculum remains crucial. The following activity is designed to help you think about these issues in more detail.

❏ Our comments

This is a difficult exercise to complete because it is often easier to identify aims and objectives than it is to see how these are translated into practice. One factor that applies to all categories is teacher (and, consequently, student) expectations, which are linked to the prevailing societal attitudes as well as personal views and ideals. We are all familiar with the notion of the 'self-fulfilling prophecy' and the impact low teacher expectations will have on students and children. The following comments, taken from *Principles for School Mathematics* (National Council of Teachers of Mathematics (USA), 2000, p. 12), are applicable to all areas of the curriculum:

Teachers communicate expectations in their interactions with students during classroom instruction, through their comments on students' papers, when assigning students to instructional groups, through the presence or absence of consistent support for students who are striving for high levels of attainment, and in their contacts with significant adults in a student's life. These actions, along with decisions and actions taken outside the classroom to assign students to different classes or curricula, also determine students' opportunities to learn and influence students' beliefs about their own abilities to succeed . . .

Activity

Equitable practice

Please consider your own institution's practice within the six categories listed below. For each category, first list what you have in place to ensure equitable practice and then note any areas for improvement. Some of your examples may relate to more than one category. You will need to refer to the list given above.

Gender	*Practice* *Improvements*
Socioeconomic status	*Practice* *Improvements*
Ethnicity	*Practice* *Improvements*
Special needs	*Practice* *Improvements*
Location	*Practice* *Improvements*
Type of school	*Practice* *Improvements*

Some common examples of how schools and colleges may try to offset the disadvantages associated with lack of equity are as follows:

- Gender-free or a choice of gender-specific examination questions.
- Providing access to computers for homework where students do not have access at home.
- Mother-tongue language support.
- The use of learning support assistants for students with special needs.
- Childcare provision.
- Transport to college – or taking college provision out to the students' neighbourhood.
- Educational visits to museums and art galleries where none exist in the immediate neighbourhood.
- Staff training to improve teaching performance.

Schools and colleges are exhorted to promote equity within a context of social, economic and political inequality and it is simplistic to expect them to compensate for factors that are not within their control. MacBeath and Mortimore (2001, p. 2) argue this should not preclude the setting of challenging targets and high expectations for all students, as 'schools can make a difference and that being in an effective as against a less effective school is a crucial determinant of the life chances for many individual young people'. In post-Pinochet Chile, this idea has led to a rethinking of the principles of equity:

> Until now, the application of the principles of equality of opportunities has insisted that all children receive a similar education; in future one must look for a differentiated education in order to achieve similar results. This implies flexibility in order to spend more resources on the schools and programmes which are attended by the poorest children, young people and adults in the countryside and the city (Garcia-Huidobro, 1990, quoted in translation in Aedo-Richmond and Richmond, 1999, p. 198).

Equity and effectiveness at an institutional level can be addressed by systems of monitoring, such as those listed below. They were written in the UK by DfE/Ofsted (1995) for schools, but could equally apply to other educational institutions and other countries:

1. How is our school currently performing?
2. Are some parts of the school more effective than others?
3. Are some groups of pupils doing better than others?
4. How does the school's performance compare with its previous achievement?
5. How does the school's performance compare with that of other schools?

Where issues of equity are concerned, answers to questions 2 and 3 will be crucial. Stoll and Fink (1996, p. 169) offer a useful comment here, which, again, can be applied to all phases of education:

> Equity is a fundamental tenet of school effectiveness. Some schools are differentially effective: they offer better opportunities to one pupil group than another, for example girls rather than boys, younger rather than older pupils, pupils of one ethnic or social class background, pupils taking particular subjects or courses, or pupils in different levels or streams. During evaluation, data should be disaggregated to examine differences between such groups.

To take an example from a college of further education:

> Once it is found, say, that engineering students have had better examination success in recent years than hairdressing trainees, that students on short, part-time courses have tended to drop out before the end, whereas those on longer, full-time courses have not, that over the past three years students working with Tutor A have done better than those working with Tutor B, that students from a particular ethnic group perform better than students from another, that the traditionally strong business studies department has actually had declining success in examinations over the past five years, then the college is in a position to address the situation (Briggs, 2002).

Following on from the principle of comparisons made at the institutional level in order to provide data that can assist in remediation of identified problems and improvement of practice across departments is the move towards comparisons between institutions or across countries. Far from promoting equity, the practice, popularly known in the UK as 'naming and shaming', can contribute to wider divisions between schools, colleges and universities, with institutions at the bottom of the 'league table' losing out on enrolments and, therefore, funding. A paper commissioned by the World Bank (2000) on equity in public examination systems lists the disadvantages and advantages of public ranking of schools on the basis of examination results alone:

Disadvantages

- Comparison between schools generally fails to take into account differences in intake and the social and physical conditions under which schools operate.

- Rankings can vary depending on the school outcome used.

- Measurement errors on which school rankings are based are seldom, if ever, taken into account when ministries of education, the media or the public are making judgements.

- Schools can manipulate pass rates by practices such as student retention and pressure on students to leave school before reaching the examination.

- Publication of school results may lead schools that are perceived to be doing well to attract students of high levels of ability, while those that are perceived to be doing badly (even though they may be 'adding' more 'value' than the perceived highly rated schools) will be left with lower-achieving students. It can also lead to the transfer of more able teachers, lower morale in individual schools and can create ghetto schools.

Advantages

It provides the following:

- An incentive for schools to perform.
- A measure that may be used for school accountability (sanctions and rewards).
- Readily interpretable information for parents and the public.

If you work in a system that employs league tables, you may wish to reflect on how far this analysis matches your own perceptions. If league tables are not part of your experience to date, you may wish to speculate on the implications for your own institution, were they to be introduced.

Further, detailed discussion of equal opportunities can be found in Coleman's chapter 'Managing for equal opportunities', in Bush and Bell (2002) *The Principles and Practice of Educational Management*. In this chapter, Coleman points out how awareness of equal opportunities influences curriculum management decisions, particularly attitudes to inclusion and the expectations of pupils.

Finally in this chapter we turn to a discussion of pedagogy, considering both its nature and the influences upon it. This prepares the ground for Chapter 2, which will look at teaching strategies and the learning environment in more detail.

The changing pedagogy

A succinct definition of pedagogy is 'the science of the art of teaching' (Loveless, 1998). This pithy phrase can be expanded to include all the interactions that take place between teacher, learner and knowledge. Another summary of pedagogy is the strategies, structures and methods for facilitating learning. The word *pedagogy* has its roots in Greek and comes from *pais*, a child, and *agogos*, leader. The literal meaning would be *to lead a child*. A related term, with which some readers may not be quite as familiar, is *andragogy*, which relates to adult learners. This word has similar roots, again from the Greek, *andros*, meaning man or adult and the distinctions, whilst clearly existing, are, to some extent, artificial, since many of the methods identified may be interchangeable, depending on which context is used as an exemplar. For example, the lecture mode is a familiar pedagogical approach to teaching adults in universities and the introduction of self-evaluation and self-directed learning into the way pupils are enabled to learn in schools is a cross-over from the andragogical approach. A perusal of the respective characteristics (Table 1.3) will illustrate some of the main distinctions that have been drawn.

Over time, pedagogy has come to be linked with the skills teachers use to instruct or impart knowledge and has, until recently, tended to ignore the contribution of the student to the process of learning and development of the knowledge base. Many teachers still call upon the pedagogical methods in use when they were at school, with minor variations in the use of materials and a nod in the direction of ICT. However, there has been an upsurge of interest in how children learn, following on the increase in knowledge of how the brain works and the conditions in which it learns most effectively. One of the main conclusions to be drawn from this brain research is that the conditions needed to promote more effective learning do not currently exist in most schools. In Chapter 2 we consider in detail models of learning and teaching and look at the current research on learning styles and their effect on teaching strategies.

One of the most significant challenges to the existing pedagogy in schools and colleges must be the technological revolution. Teachers have been ousted from their position as the 'gatekeepers' of knowledge with the advent of the Internet and the rapid expansion of modern telecommunication capability. This shift in the way students may now gain access to knowledge could be construed as a threat or as an opportunity for teachers to identify new possibilities that go beyond the traditional pedagogy. Loveless (1995) sees ICT as 'having the potential to act as a catalyst for the interaction between teacher, learner and knowledge' and also to change the contexts in which teachers practise through the development of flexible learning spaces. She believes that

> ICT can enhance existing pedagogy, from providing opportunities to develop compositions in writing to developing graphic skills. The presence of the ICT resources and applications in themselves are not sufficient to promote or challenge understanding, and effective capability with ICT depends not on skills, but on the context in which the experience is embedded (Loveless, 1998, p. 4).

Table 1.3 Characteristics of pedagogical and andragogical approaches

	Pedagogical	Andragogical
The learner	• The learner is dependent on the instructor for learning • The teacher/instructor assumes full responsibility for what is taught and how it is learned • The teacher/instructor evaluates learning	• The learner is self-directed • The learner is responsible for his or her own learning • Self-evaluation is characteristic of this approach
Role of the learner's experience	• The learner comes to the activity with little experience that could be tapped as a resource for learning • The experience of the instructor is what counts	• Learner brings a greater volume and quality of experience • Adults are the richest resources for one another • Different experiences assure diversity in groups of adults • Experience becomes the source of self-identity
• Readiness to learn	• Students are told what they have to learn in order to advance to the next level of mastery	• Any change is likely to trigger a readiness to learn • The *need to know* in order to perform more effectively in some aspect of one's life • Ability to assess gaps between where one is now and where one wants and needs to be
Orientation to learning	• Learning as a process of acquiring prescribed subject matter • Content units are sequenced according to the logic of the subject matter	• Learners want to perform a task, solve a problem, live in a more satisfying way • Must have relevance to these tasks • Learning is organised around life/work situations rather than subject-matter units
• Motivation for learning	• Primarily motivated by *external* pressures, competition for grades and the consequences of failure	• *Internal* motivators: self-esteem, recognition, better quality of life, self-confidence, self-actualisation

Source: Yale University Library (2000).

In other words, teachers now need to become responsible for harnessing the potential of ICT to enhance the learning experience of their students. This responsibility carries with it the challenge that faces all reforms: how to ensure the effective 'old' methods are not lost in the enthusiasm for the new. To use the idea of promoting emotional intelligence (Goleman, 1995) as an example, teachers are unlikely to be successful in developing this in their students by means of an instruction programme delivered through a computer.

Activity

Identifying the impact of ICT

Drawing upon your own experience, reflect on the ways teaching methods have changed in response to the introduction of ICT into schools and colleges. In terms of the management of learning and teaching in its broadest sense (to include curriculum management), how has ICT changed practice?

❑ Our comments

The impact of ICT will be moderated by availability and teacher expertise. Institutions will obviously differ in the extent to which they have access to modern technology and, consequently, the uses to which it may be put. Students will also vary in this respect, with some being provided with a personal computer at home for their exclusive use, with others coming from homes with no access. There are obvious questions about equality of opportunity to be answered.

The data-handling capacity of ICT has revolutionised the keeping of assessment records and their analysis for the purposes of accountability and reporting. The use of presentation software or interactive whiteboards in the classroom can give an edge to didactive teaching that engages students more actively than the traditional 'chalk and talk'. Computer networking allows the teacher to provide differentiated work programmes, which more closely match the ability and pace of individual students. There are many more examples.

The use of ICT to enhance learning and teaching will be considered in greater detail in the next chapter within the section on the virtual learning environment, but it is useful to note here the impact the World Wide Web has had on life-long learning. The adult learner, outside formal educational structures, will, typically, engage in self-directed learning and has the opportunity to access the vast knowledge base now available as a result of the technological revolution in a way unparalleled in history. The NACCCE Report (1999, p. 21) makes the point forcefully when it says:

> The real long-term effects of the revolution in information technology have still to be felt. The rate of technological change is quickening every day. Information technologies are transforming how we think, how we work and how we play. The new frontiers created by nano-technology and extreme miniaturisation promise a wholly new era of information systems.

Although the authors of the report note that young people are 'often more alert to the possibilities of new technologies' than adults, they are also acquiring skills that will continue to be used and developed throughout adult life. At the same time, adults in a wide variety of contexts are having continually to improve their skills in order to meet the demands of work and leisure. Learning, therefore, is not only part of the expectations of the specialised workplace but is increasingly seen as a desirable activity in all walks of life.

Any discussion of the 'technological revolution' within the context of life-long learning does tend to assume universal access to adequately resourced educational opportunities when, of course, this is far from true for the vast majority, even in developed countries. This problem is clearly identified in The Ocho Rios Declaration (2001, p. 1) of the International Council for Adult Education when they say:

an international consensus has been reached on the right to education and the right to learn throughout life for women and men as well as on the central role of adult education in support of creative and demo-cratic citizenship . . . [but] We are caught in a dilemma between the possibilities of a genuinely democratic and sustainable learning society, and the passivity, poverty, vulnerability and chaos that economic globali-sation is creating everywhere.

❑ **Key learning points**

- Curriculum is a concept that refers to everything that happens in a school: what is taught and what is learnt, what is included and what is left out.

- National curricula arise out of the cultural, political and social context as a way of preserv-ing (or creating) the identity of different groups.

- Globalisation and the technical revolution contribute to curricular similarities between countries, although national preferences or economic imperatives ensure diversity.

- learning and teaching are the core business of schools and colleges, but institutions will vary in how they organise these. Pedagogical approaches are changing in response to influences such as learning theory and ICT developments.

- There is a growing number of stakeholders who exert various degrees of influence over the curriculum. However, external control is mitigated by the 'personalising' influence of teachers in the classroom.

- The culture and values of an institution underpin the principles (as expressed in policy statements) and practices (as observed in classrooms). Culture is not a f ed state but dependent on the collective influences of all stakeholders.

- As the gap between rich and poor continues to grow, the issue of equity in education becomes more pressing. Access to high-quality education, far from being a universal right, is restricted by both economic and ideological factors.

2. Managing the context of learning

Introduction

In this chapter we consider the all-important topics of learning and teaching, and we consider some of the environments in which they take place. This should enable us as researchers and managers to gain insight into the processes underlying learning and teaching and to understand better how they can be managed. It is difficult to make meaningful generalisations about curriculum provision, especially on an international basis; as Woodhead (1999, p. 115) comments when reporting on research visits to early years programmes in Venezuela, India, Turkey, Kenya and France:

> 'The general label "Early Childhood Programme" encompassed profound contrasts: in organisation, financing, buildings, facilities and equipment; staff training and ratios; approach to care and education; relative emphasis on health, nutrition, play and thinking, social learning pre-academic skills; and relationships to family and community.'

Variations in the factors listed here – finance, approach to education, relationships of education with family and community – will affect directly or indirectly the investigation of the context of learning in any phase of education, and the norms by which researchers and practitioners will first be guided are the norms for their own country. Considering the experiences of practitioners in other countries and other phases of education can be illuminating and thought-provoking, but that does not mean it is possible or appropriate to transfer practice directly from one culture to another. This text as a whole, and this chapter in particular, is underpinned by that understanding. We hope the frameworks of thought offered, and the examples given, will be useful in constructing your own sets of concepts for analysis and for identifying examples of good practice within your own working context.

At whatever level you are managing the curriculum, an understanding of the processes of learning and teaching is essential. Dimmock (2000) illustrates this vividly in Figure 2.1 when he demonstrates how a school or college that is learning centred might be designed on the basis of a whole-institution focus upon learning outcomes. Following the arrows from the base of the diagram, consideration of the desired student outcomes guides the planning of the process and content of the learning activities, which in turn influence teaching methods and strategies. These affect the way in which the school or college is structured and organised. The last link in the sequence is therefore to design the type of leadership, management, resources and culture that will effectively support the structures, the teaching, the learning and the learning outcomes. Instead of the learning outcome being the 'product' of all the elements above it in the diagram, the outcomes actually shape the nature of the elements above, and therefore the institution itself.

Figure 2.1   The learning-centred school
Source: Dimmock (2000, p. 27)

This chapter will attempt to address the three elements that appear at the bottom of Figure 2.1 through a consideration of learning, of teaching and of managing the contexts in which they take place. In the next chapter discussion of the various management roles and structures will enable you to consider some aspects of the other two elements.

Models of learning and teaching

The 'mirror' activities of learning and teaching have received much attention of recent years in many countries. Advances in understanding, both of the processes of the mind and of the impact of social and cultural factors upon learning, have led to a greater interest in assessing the conditions under which learning is taking place. Where there is a strong tradition of learning and teaching by means of particular classroom strategies, to which both learners and teachers are accustomed and committed, these strategies are likely to be valued and successful.

Where schools and colleges are working with learners who do not relate well to learning by accustomed methods and who may be mistrustful of them, a useful approach is to highlight the variety of learning needs among the students and to adopt what is termed an inclusive approach, which addresses the breadth of learning needs presented. In the case of specialist schools and colleges, catering for students of a particular ability range or offering particular subject specialisms, there will also be pressure to understand better how students learn in those specialist contexts in order to meet the aspirations embodied in the institution. This in turn will influence the models of teaching adopted.

Other potentially influential factors, in countries where education is to any extent market driven, include the concept of the student as a customer or client whose learning needs should be assessed and who should be involved in the management of his or her own learning. In post-compulsory education, retaining students on their courses through to completion is an important factor, both in obtaining funding for the college and in managing its reputation in an 'open' market. There are commonly systems of accountability for both schools and colleges that demand visible – and ever-improving –

success in public examinations. These last two pressures influence the way schools and colleges examine how their students can best be encouraged to stay, to learn and to succeed in their examinations.

Models of teaching are therefore strongly influenced both by *the prevailing culture of the education system* and the *generic and particular needs of the learner*. Where rote learning is the norm and is an accustomed route towards understanding, it is adopted and valued; where children learn well through engagement with a practical task, this is a preferred approach; where learning a skill is commonly undertaken and assessed 'on the job' in an adult working environment, this is an appropriate model. However, from time to time teachers and managers identify the need for change in models of teaching, which may also necessitate changes in the ways in which teaching is viewed and valued. This may well involve a reassessment of aims and strategies, a moving away from the 'comfort zone' of current practice; there may be a lengthy period of debate and of partial adoption and evaluation of a new system before it is fully accepted and fully effective. Change takes both time and careful management, and alterations to curriculum delivery are constrained by many factors, internal and external to the institution; therefore in many schools and colleges there may be a disparity between what is known and understood about learning, and what actually happens in the classroom.

Activity

Changing models

Before going on to read about models of learning and of teaching, try to assess whether there are pressures upon you and your institution to change your models of teaching. If there are no pressures to change, ask yourself how far the models adopted suit the needs of the present learners. If change is evident, what is driving it? Is it the needs of the learner, the needs of the organisation or some local or national government directive?

❑ Our comments

A stable situation may be just that – stable and suitable to the needs of the majority. You will read below about learner expectations, and your system may be driven by what learners expect and are accustomed to.

If there are pressures for change, they may be influenced by the needs of any or all the parties listed above: the learner, the organisation, local or national government. You will read below about research into learning styles that helps us to understand the needs of the learner; about whether the organisation of the school or college is driven by the provision of a satisfactory learning experience for the students, or whether the learning experience is shaped by the imperatives of institutional organisation; and lastly about instances where government directives have shaped the learning experience of the child. As you read, you may be able to understand your own situation better and see ways of managing the change for the benefit of the learner.

Learning styles

In this section we shall examine some of the recent research and thinking about how people learn. In many educational systems, these developments have influenced – or are starting to influence – models of teaching.

One of the researchers who has most influenced thinking in this field is Howard Gardner; in his work on *multiple intelligences* (1983), he defines seven 'intelligences' that, he argues, are possessed by each person in different proportions:

- Logical-mathematical
- Linguistic
- Spatial
- Bodily kinaesthetic
- Musical
- Interpersonal
- Intrapersonal.

These categories of intelligence are based upon 'evidence on the biological origins of problem-solving ability and the ways in which such abilities are expressed and developed in the world' (Bentley, 1998, p. 22). Gardner argues that learners can be enabled to make best use of their blend of intelligences when teaching styles address five entry points that lead to understanding:

1. The narrational or story-telling approach

2. The logical-quantitative approach

3. The foundational or philosophical approach

4. The aesthetic approach

5. The experiential approach.

These 'entry points' suggest a range of teaching environments that could be available to the learner. For example: a classroom with chairs and desks focused upon the teacher would facilitate a narrational approach; a learning area that could provide stimuli from music or art would encourage an aesthetic approach; interactive learning environments – outside the classroom, in the workplace or on a computer-based intranet – could provide a setting for an experiential approach.

Other researchers have proposed different analyses of the learning process, all pointing to the proposition that learners need to experience a range of stimuli and strategies for learning. For example, McCarthy and her colleagues (1990) have devised a '4MAT' system of assessing learning styles and of structuring the method and the content of the curriculum to allow for differences in the ways people both *perceive* and *process* knowledge. The theory behind the system is based on right mode/left mode preferences in the brain, proposing that some people *perceive* in concrete ways by sensing and feeling; others perceive in abstract ways by thinking things through and reflection. In *processing* information, some people are watchers first, others are doers. When the methods of perception and processing are superimposed upon each other (Figure 2.2), four different learning styles are identified:

Type 1: imaginative learners.
Type 2: analytic learners.
Type 3: commonsense learners.
Type 4: dynamic learners.

Models of teaching that 'play to the strengths' learners have identified or that encourage them to co-operate with learners who use different strategies can be developed once the learners' predominant styles have been assessed.

Figure 2.2 4MAT analysis of learning styles
Source: McCarthy (1990), adapted by Dimmock (2000, p. 120)

As a result of the growing interest in learning styles, self-assessment questionnaires on the subject are now commonplace. Some are adapted from *experiential learning theory* (Kolb, 1985), from analysis of team roles (Belbin, 1981) or from research into *cognitive styles of learning* (Riding, 1991). Honey and Mumford (1986) focus on *social approaches to learning*; their questionnaires – available for both teenage and mature learners – enable students to construct learning profiles on the basis of their relative strengths as activists, reflectors, theorists and pragmatists.

The sensory analysis of learning styles, following work by Reinert (1976), has stimulated educational writers and publishers (e.g. Keefe, 1989; Byatt and Davies, 1998) to produce materials that not only promote self-analysis but also give direct advice on study strategies to the learner. In this type of analysis, learners are helped to assess their own preferred sensory learning style on the basis they process information through visual, auditory and kinaesthetic channels and may have individual preferences for which channels they use. Having analysed predominant channels for processing information, the learner is offered guidelines for application. If the tutor has access to the analysis, teaching styles can be adapted to suit the predominant needs of the group and to have regard for the needs of individuals. For further examples of learning style models, a recent review can be found in Riding and Raynor (1999) on page 76.

Research by Goleman (1996) into *emotional intelligence*, based on work by Salovey and Mayer (1990), has added a further perspective to the educational process. Salovey and Mayer identify five major domains of emotional intelligence:

1. Knowing one's emotions

2. Managing emotions

3. Motivating oneself

4. Recognising emotions in others

5. Handling relationships.

They maintain that people's personal strengths and strategies and interactions with others will be governed by the balance of these domains within them. Goleman (1996) proposes that emotional intelligence is a crucial factor in determining a person's life chances. He underlines the importance of children's development of emotional intelligence, which can provide the child, and subsequently the adult, with personal qualities that form the basis of successful social interactions. He proposes that the negative effects of emotional trauma in children can be reduced by developing the more positive elements in their emotional portfolio, and that social intelligence can be developed to counterbalance an innate disposition, for example, to shyness.

Emotional 'illiteracy', Goleman maintains, is costly both to the individual and society, and can be prevented. Whilst the main development of emotional competence takes place within the family, educationists can see that schools and colleges have a role to play here: 'Developing emotional literacy is obviously a crucial part of preparing young people to survive and succeed in adult life, and Goleman's work provides powerful evidence that schools can play an important part, though not an exclusive one, in supporting it' (Bentley, 1998, p. 26). It is widely proposed in western educational settings (Stephenson, 1992; Gibbs *et al.*, 1994; Hodkinson, 1994) that active learning – where the learner takes control of solving a problem or achieving a goal – at its most effective results in 'deep learning', where concepts are deeply understood and are of lasting benefit to the individual. Fazey (1996, p. 30) points out that active learning is not achievable without guidance; the teacher or guidance worker has an active role to play: 'Active decision-making has to be accompanied by expert guidance if the learner is to achieve the desired destination.' In a UK context, active learning might involve intensive use of resource-based learning, where the student or pupil – individually or in groups – uses a range of resources in order to investigate a defined area of the curriculum. In Chinese and Asian cultures (Dimmock, 2000), rote learning might be involved, with memorisation and repetition being used as strategies for deep learning. In both cases, the purpose of the learning activity would have to be understood in order for the learner to conceptualise from the experience.

A cross-cultural perspective

The final example given above leads us to a consideration of culture as an important factor in the management of learning and teaching. The learning models described above, like most analyses of learning, are based upon Western educational traditions. In the following section we analyse some differences in educational traditions that affect the ways in which learning and teaching are viewed. The cultures chosen for comparison here are those that may loosely be termed 'Western' and those that might be considered as 'Confucian', sometimes referred to in the literature specifically as Chinese. Approaches to education in your country may fall neatly into one of these categories; if they do not, we hope the examples offered here will enable you to recognise and analyse the approaches to learning and teaching that underpin your own educational system. The following section draws strongly on Watkins' (2000) meta-analysis of published and unpublished research, which enabled comparison of approaches to learning in eight Western and eight non-Western countries.

> *Memorisation*, including repetition, is a learning technique that is out of favour in some western education systems. It is often associated with rote learning – memorising without understanding – and not considered to lead to deep learning. Watkins (2000, pp. 163–14) reports on research that found that for students in the Chinese school systems in Hong Kong, repetition 'was associated with creating a "deep impression", and thence with memorisation'. Repetition was also 'used to deepen or develop understanding by discovering new meaning' (ibid.). Students in the Western school systems of Hong Kong used repetition to 'to check that they had really remembered something'.

Another difference perceived by Watkins and Biggs (1996) is the *learner's concept of ability*. They report that Chinese students – and their teachers and parents – regard ability as something that can be improved by hard work rather than as something innate and relatively unchangeable. This affects the value placed on student effort within the school system, compared with the valuing of sudden insight: 'Whereas the Western students saw understanding as usually a process of sudden insights, Chinese students typically thought of understanding as a long process that required considerable mental effort' (Watkins, 2000, p. 166).

The *underlying culture of the country* as valuing either individual or collective achievement also has an effect upon the motivation of the learner. Western societies are characterised by individualism where the need for success tries to overcome the fear of failure (Atkinson, 1964) and achievement is generally seen as ego-enhancing; in east Asian societies, success is seen in a collectivist context, which includes family, peers and even society as a whole (Holloway, 1988; Salili 1996). The concept of 'family face' (Ho, 1993), where studying hard is a responsibility to the family (Lee, 1996), has a strong effect on motivation. The valuing of collective achievement may also lead to supportive student–student relationships. For example, Jin and Cortazzi (1998) report high levels of mutual student support and a corresponding lack of teasing in their study of classrooms in Japan and China.

The *collective approach to learning*, combined with the ability to memorise purposefully, may underlie differences observed by Jin and Cortazzi (ibid.) in the way group work was used by western and Chinese teachers. In western classrooms, group work was usually simultaneous – the whole class split into groups or pairs to discuss a problem together. In Chinese classrooms, group work – or more often pair work – was sequential: pupils carried out a discursive dialogue to which the rest of the class listened and responded internally, knowing that another pair would soon be selected to continue the dialogue. The authors consider this Chinese approach is cognitive centred, compared with the largely skills-centred approach of western group work.

Jin and Cortazzi (1998) also offer insight into differences of *perception of what is a 'good teacher'* among British and Chinese secondary school students. The British students valued teachers who could arouse their interest, explain clearly and use a range of effective teaching methods and learning activities. They liked teachers who were patient and sympathetic when students did not understand. The Chinese valued the deep knowledge possessed by the 'good teacher', and the teacher's ability to answer questions and set a moral example, whilst at the same time being warm and friendly inside and outside the classroom.

Watkins (2000, p. 168) sums up the Confucian principles that underpin the observations offered in this section:

- The high value placed on education by society
- That learning involves reflection and application
- That hard work compensates for lack of ability
- That the teacher is a model both of knowledge and morality
- That learning is a moral duty and studying hard is a responsibility to the family.

The evaluation of the 'good teacher' offered below by UK Year 8 pupils, quoted in the Hay McBer report (DfEE, 2000, Introduction), illustrates the attributes noted above as being valued by 'western' learners, but also illustrates the warmth and approachability expected of teachers in both cultures. A good teacher . . .

is kind
is generous
listens to you
encourages you
has faith in you
keeps confidences
likes teaching children
likes teaching their subject
takes time to explain things
helps you when you're stuck
tells you how you are doing
allows you to have your say
doesn't give up on you
cares for your opinion
makes you feel clever
treats people equally
stands up for you
makes allowances
tells the truth
is forgiving.

From these summaries we can see that the attitudes and expectations of society as a whole, as well as those of the individual learner, affect how learning is viewed and how teaching is organised. These attitudes and expectations vary from country to country, and attempts to 'graft' learning and teaching concepts from one society into another may therefore not be successful.

Teaching strategies

Looking at the range of learning theories available – and the number of expectations upon teachers – in order to consider appropriate teaching strategies, may seem a bewildering task for teachers and managers. However, the individual reflective practitioner and the manager with responsibility for a curriculum team are both likely to review and evaluate teaching strategies on a regular basis in order to maintain quality of learning and teaching. There is little evidence that focusing on one particular theory of learning styles and incorporating it into teaching strategies produces measurable improvement in learning (Stahl, 1999; Muijs and Reynolds, 2001). What is evident is that, as Joyce and Showers (1991, p. 10) observe, 'Outstanding schools teach their students ways of learning. Thus, teaching becomes more effective as students progress through those schools because, year by year, the students have been taught to be stronger learners'. How is this to be achieved?

A large-scale study of current and withdrawn students at colleges of further education in England by Martinez and Munday (1998) recommends, among other things, that early difficulties with course work, which can be a symptom of students failing to settle in successfully, could be addressed by 'initial development of study skills' and 'diagnosis of learning styles'. Similarly, where the problems develop during the programme, 'varied and stimulating teaching strategies' are suggested as a possible solution. Two of the factors that encourage students to stay and succeed are the student's awareness of their own learning process and the lecturer's response to the varied learning needs of the group.

The Tomlinson report (1996, p. 4) into strategies for inclusiveness in post-compulsory learning in the UK places an emphasis on the teacher being aware of the students' learning styles, and adapting teaching styles and learning materials to meet their needs: 'We must move . . . towards creating an appropriate learning environment; concentrate on understanding better how people learn so that they can be better helped to learn . . . redesigning the very processes of learning, assessment and organisation so as to fit the objectives and learning styles of the students.'

The focus on learning itself, through the 'learning conversations' that take place between tutor and student when learning styles analysis is undertaken, can serve to increase motivation, both in the tutor and the student (Briggs, 1999). Dimmock (2000, p. 123), after warning that teachers are likely to adopt teaching styles that are dependent on their own learning styles, suggests that: 'Teachers can work towards equity for all students by developing flexible and adaptable teaching styles. Thus teachers should provide a variety of options and choices to meet the same goals and objectives in lessons and course units so that students with different learning styles can all be engaged.'

Where student and pupil motivation for learning is high, the choices of teaching strategies adopted may have a less crucial influence on success. MacBeath and Mortimore (2001, p. 15) refer to work by Reynolds and Farrell (1996) identifying cultural factors that can make a difference to pupil and student achievement:

- The high status of teachers and the recruitment of high achieving students into teaching

- Religious traditions and cultural aspirations that place a high value on learning

- Confucian beliefs on the role of effort, striving and working hard

- High aspirations of parents for their children

- High levels of commitment from children to do well

- The prevalent belief that all children can acquire core skills.

In many 'high-achieving countries', such as Singapore, Hong Kong and Taiwan, according to MacBeath and Mortimore (2001), class sizes are large, and the opportunities for variety in teaching styles are few, but the strong features of national, community or home culture listed here and discussed in the previous section are likely to be influential upon success.

In the reading and discussion that follow, teaching strategies are analysed through a series of broad 'approaches'. We hope you will find these helpful in analysing practice at your own institution.

 Reading

Please read the chapter 'Models of curriculum organisation' by Peter Silcock and Mark Brundrett, Chapter 3 in Middlewood, D. and Burton, N. (2001) *Managing the Curriculum*.

As you read, think which of the three approaches to learning and teaching are in operation at your school or college.

❏ Our comments
The following section explores some of the ideas raised in the chapter.

❏ *Teacher-centred approaches*
In this model, the teacher holds the power in the teaching–learning relationship. Teacher-centred models may be adopted as a technique for pupil management where class sizes are high and in cultures where there is a tradition of the 'knowledgeable teacher' from whom the learners seek insight and understanding. Research in secondary schools in the Shaanxi Province of China by Bush *et al.* (1998, p. 189) reported class sizes of up to 75 pupils – although 50 was more typical – where 'whole class teaching

predominates, using the traditional modes of learning, recitation and review'. However, the researchers concluded that in the Chinese schools 'large classes and formal approaches do not appear to be inimical to high standards' (ibid.). In this example, tradition plays a part in the pedagogy: this is how the pupils expect to learn and the teachers expect to teach. Similarly, the large formal lecture is probably still a prominent – and expected – feature of university undergraduate teaching in many countries: the influences of tradition and pragmatism both play a part here, even though western educational systems do not generally prepare learners to learn well through this mode.

As Silcock and Brundrett (2001) point out, teacher-centred approaches are based on control and are adopted where the level of teacher knowledge is high and where there are clearly defined targets for learning. This approach may therefore be favoured in vocational education, where specific technical and craft-based techniques need to be passed on to trainees. Student numbers may not necessarily be high in this case: learning may take place through intensive one-to-one sessions in the workplace between apprentice and trainer.

In school systems where a national curriculum is tightly defined and test results are given prominence, teachers may find themselves 'teaching to the test' using a teacher-centred approach. A comment from a teacher in England, reported by Helsby (1999, p. 78), illustrates this: 'National Curriculum assessment means that you are teaching more to the test or exam, there's a loss of flexibility. The investigative approach in science is laid down in a particular way in the National Curriculum . . . it's become so rigid and formalised.' The teacher here was clearly feeling the loss of a teaching style that was formerly valued: it is ironic that in the 'investigative approach' referred to – a pedagogic approach that might normally be deemed learner centred – neither the learners nor the teachers were driving the process; instead, the teachers were acting as agents within an externally devised scheme.

❏ *Learner-centred approaches*
In this model, the learner holds the power: 'Student- or learner-centred schools, whilst much discussed in concept and praised in terms of approach, are rare in reality' (Wagner, 2000, p. 373, based on Banathy, 1993). Wagner goes on to discuss this paradox in terms that are helpful to us here. Taking the issue of control highlighted above by Silcock and Brundrett, she claims the organisational infrastructure of schools, based on traditional arrangements and policies, is not designed for learning but rather for control (Wagner, 2000, p. 375, citing Dale, 1997, p. 36). She highlights the rationale of Dimmock (2000), exemplified in this book in Figure 2.1, that the core technology of the school – the learning and teaching process – should drive the organisational structures rather than the other way around.

So, can learner-centred approaches succeed? Wagner (2000, p. 384) claims they can in such specialised learning environments as the Montessori system, which she describes as 'vision-led, principle-guided and process driven [i.e. the learning process]', and she speculates whether success in this system is partly also a function of the size of the institution and its primary/elementary level. A feature of special schools is their learner-centred approach, based on individual programmes and small group teaching.

Dimmock (2000, pp. 20–21) describes the characteristics of a learning-centred school, where learners and learning are placed at the heart of school activity. Having regard for the influences of different cultures on learning, he uses terms he considers are not culture-dependent:

- Student outcomes are converted into meaningful learning goals for individual students
- Every student is valued as a learner
- Relevant information is collected on each student's learning characteristics and achievements
- Research findings are sought on effective learning principles as guides to practice

- Wherever possible, school-wide policies and shared practices on learning are adopted for consistency and reinforcement
- The whole school is viewed as a learning community.

Silcock and Brundrett (2001, p. 39) define learner-centred approaches as those where the tutor guides and facilitates the learners, rather than asserting control, towards targeted learning goals; they argue these approaches are most common in primary and post-compulsory education. They warn managers that these approaches have associated practical problems such as complex record-keeping, and that they are resource-hungry. Dimmock (2000, p. 123) advocates offering a range of learning options and choices in order for group members to meet learning goals: this certainly implies a broad range of resources in different media. More mature and motivated learners may resource themselves; others may depend upon the ingenuity of their teachers.

❑ *Partnership approaches*

In this model, power is shared between learner and teacher. Silcock and Brundrett (2001, p. 44) describe partnership approaches as those that 'recognise that successful education demands a fruitful collaboration between the teachers and learners, where each has complementary roles, rather than one being subsidiary to the other'. They emphasise the principle of democracy that underpins such approaches: this democracy may extend not only to students but to parents and communities as well.

A partnership approach may also encompass the notion of schools and colleges as learning communities, 'where everyone (students, teachers, parents, administrators) is both a learner and a teacher, dependent upon circumstances (Clarke, 2000, p. 27). People working in such an organisation, where the principal or headteacher is the 'leading learner' (Southworth, 1994, p. 53), may be in a position to understand the requirements of its pupil or student learners to manage the institution's systems in such a way as to enable learning to happen and to respond to the needs of individual learners.

Silcock and Brundrett (2001, p. 47) see the partnership approach as one where teachers are still 'gate-keepers' of knowledge, but where they set up systems where 'curricula can be explored imaginatively and critically by teachers and students alike'. It is an approach where learners both become politically empowered and also have their concepts of what has been learned challenged and debated so that learning can be applied and understood more deeply. Within the classroom, an example of this approach would be the 'inquiry teaching style' defined by Sorenson *et al.* (1988), presented in Dimmock (2000, p. 122):

> The teacher forms a partnership with the students as individuals, pairs or in small groups. The teacher presents ideas to stimulate students to think and problem solve. The lesson often starts in a large class, and eventually breaks into small groups to raise and address questions and to collect data necessary in the research process. Each student has a clearly defined role in the enquiry team, and these roles may be rotated.

In considering the concept of partnership as extending beyond the institution, Stoll and Fink (1996, p. 134) describe the web of relationships schools have: 'all the individuals, groups, organisations and institutions which share responsibility for the growth and development of pupils'. They also maintain that schools need 'critical friends': 'individuals and groups who, at appropriate times, listen and help them to sort out their thinking and make sound decisions, who are not afraid to tell them when expectations for themselves are too low and when their actions do not meet their expectations'.

Stoll and Fink are writing here in a school context: this kind of partnership may be even more prevalent at the level of post-compulsory education. Colleges offering academic and vocational programmes will of necessity work in partnership with local and national organisations and agencies, which perform an advisory or monitoring role in relation to curriculum provision.

Lumby (2001b, p. 123), writing about further education, says:

> In many ways students cannot make decisions about their learning. It would not be possible to have an entirely different qualification for every student. The content and assessment of particular programmes may be agreed at regional or national level. Industry standards must be upheld. Some common skills are needed. Students may have insufficient knowledge to make informed choices about what is appropriate preparation for a particular vocation or role. A more realistic aim may be one of shared control where the learner can influence the nature of his or her learning more than previously, but there is still a need for partnership . . .

Partnerships may serve to strengthen, rather than dilute, the capacity of the teacher and the learner to manage and benefit from the learning process.

❑ *Inclusive approaches*

Power in this model is retained by the teacher and the organisation, but the strength of the inclusive philosophy that stresses that the needs of the learner should be identified and addressed means the power is used benevolently for the benefit of the learner. In her chapter 'Managing individual needs within an inclusive curriculum' (Chapter 10 of *Managing the Curriculum*), Daniela Sommefeldt writes about the movement towards inclusiveness in the UK and other countries. This approach focuses on the needs of students who have special educational needs, whether through physical or learning disability, but the philosophy readily extends to regarding all students as individuals with different learning needs and placing the onus upon the college or school to identify and meet those needs. Writing of the Tomlinson report, *Inclusive Learning* (1996), which reported upon provision for students in further education with disabilities or learning difficulties, Sommefeldt (2001, p. 156) comments:

> The most significant aspect of the report is the view that difficulty or deficit should not be seen to reside in the individual, but within the institution, leading to the expectation that colleges will increase their capacity to respond to the needs of the individual learners. This is described as an 'individual learning environment'.

This report was seminal within the UK further education sector, initiating college-wide 'inclusiveness' audits and numerous investigative projects that focused upon strategies for meeting the needs of individual learners.

In reporting on data from 19 member countries on practices that maximise interaction between disabled and non-disabled pupils, the OECD (1995) identified the following key features (cited in Sommefeldt, 2001, p. 161):

- Access to the curriculum via buildings/equipment and pedagogy
- School organisation which is flexible and supportive
- Staff training at all levels to develop the necessary skills and attitudes
- Working with parents to enable involvement in their children's education.

Two further features out of those highlighted by the OECD (1995, p. 193) as supporting successful integration are of particular interest here:

- Catering for individuals, rather than just offering standard programmes
- Recognising social and life skills, as well as academic achievement, as contributing to the success of the school.

If you work in programmes of adult basic education, or 'return to learn' programmes, you may well recognise your own philosophy here. One characteristic of these models is the positive classroom climate they aim to create: a feature we return to later in this chapter in the section 'Classroom climate'.

What these recommendations, both by Tomlinson and the OECD, are pointing to is an approach that is learner centred but not necessarily learner directed. Many of the students being considered here will not be able to take charge of their own learning but will depend upon the experience, insight and flexibility of teachers and managers to make provision for their needs.

❑ *Effectiveness approaches*

A fuller discussion of the literature of school effectiveness and school improvement can be found in one of the partner 'core texts' in this series: *Leadership and Strategic Management in Schools and Colleges* (Bush and Coleman, 2000). In this text we think it is useful to consider some of the aspects of school effectiveness – factors that promote greater student progress in one institution than another – within the context of the management of learning and teaching in the classroom. Considering the list of 11 factors contributing to effectiveness, from Sammons *et al.* (1995, p. 8), quoted on page 48 of Bush and Coleman (2000), we find that, whilst all the factors impact upon learning and teaching, some focus directly upon classroom relationships. For convenience, the whole list is reproduced here:

1. *Professional leadership*
   Firm and purposeful
   A participative approach
   The leading professional

2. *Shared vision and goals*
   Unity of purpose
   Consistency of practice
   Collegiality and collaboration

3. *A learning environment*
   An orderly atmosphere
   An attractive working environment

4. *Concentration on learning and teaching*
   Maximisation of learning time
   Academic emphasis
   Focus on achievement

5. *High expectations*
   High expectations all round
   Communicating expectations
   Providing intellectual challenge

6. *Positive reinforcement*
   Clear and fair discipline
   Feedback

7. *Monitoring progress*
   Monitoring pupil performance
   Evaluating school performance

8. *Pupil rights and responsibilities*
   High pupil self-esteem
   Positions of responsibility
   Control of work

9. *Purposeful teaching*
   Efficient organisation
   Clarity of purpose
   Structured lessons
   Adaptive practice

10. *A learning organisation*
    School-based staff development

11. *Home–school partnership*
    Parental involvement.

The list is offered in the context of primary and secondary schools: most of the elements will easily 'translate' and transfer to further education, and many to early years and special school provision.

Many aspects of element 3 'A learning environment' are considered more fully in the next section of this book. Here we focus on the 'orderly atmosphere' of this learning environment, which links with aspects of other elements, such as 'clear and fair discipline' and 'efficient organisation' to give the impression of a controlled and purposeful learning situation. This would normally be created through teacher control – perhaps suggesting a teacher-centred model – but element 8 'Pupil rights and responsibilities' indicates that control, once established, can be shared with the learners, indicating a partnership approach. Certainly, as learners become older, and particularly in the post-compulsory phase of education, the control and the purpose are achieved increasingly through the motivation and autonomous status of the students themselves.

Element 4 'Concentration on learning and teaching' needs to be set within the context of Chapter 1 of this text (i.e. that an appropriate curriculum is being offered and that the learners' needs are being met). 'Academic emphasis' may not be appropriate to some phases of education, but making the best use of learning time and having a focus on achievement – whether it is social, academic or vocational – is important. We would add 'enjoyment of learning' – on the part of both teacher and learner – to the descriptors of the element. Enjoyment stimulates engagement with learning and is a strong motivating factor.

Elements 5 and 6 'High expectations' and 'Positive reinforcement' echo the motto of the Glasser Institute in the USA (Glasser, 2000): 'Every student can learn.' 'High expectations all round' indicates learners should have high expectations of themselves and each other: this attitude, although initiated by the teacher or by the culture of the school or college, needs to be adopted by the pupils and students themselves. We will return to the issue of positive and negative expectations in the section on 'Classroom climate' below.

'Purposeful teaching', combined with 'Monitoring progress' – elements 9 and 7, respectively – indicate a model of teaching that has clear aims, clear understanding of how the aims are to be met and effective evaluation of the extent to which the aims are being met and learning is taking place. Increasingly with older students, these aims would be transparent and shared with the learners so that the learners can better understand and monitor their own progress. The topic of evaluation is further discussed in Chapter 3 of this text.

What emerges strongly from Sammons' analysis is a model of learning and teaching based on clarity of focus, purposefulness of approach, high expectations and high learner self-esteem. Whatever the phase of education under consideration, this could be a good model to aspire to.

❏ *Aspirational approaches*

The recent turn of the millennium provided a tempting opportunity for writers to reconfigure institutions imaginatively in 'third millennium' terms in an attempt to resolve some of the unmet needs of the second. The following list, offered by Clarke (2000, p. 49), drawing on work by Townsend *et al.* (1999), addresses many of the issues concerning learning and teaching we have been considering so far, together with some to be considered in the next section. Clarke (2000) writes within the context of schools, but many of his aspirations fit equally well – if not better – into the college context. In his 'vision' for the third millennium:

- People have access to learning 24 hours a day, 365 days a year, through a variety of sources.

- Teachers are employed to match teaching to the needs of the learner.

- Schools are learning communities where everyone (students, teachers, parents, administrators) is both a learner and a teacher, depending on circumstances.

- Information is accessed according to the learner's capability and interest. The information varies greatly after basic skills are learned.

- Schools as we know them have been dramatically altered in form and function, or have been replaced.

- Communities are responsible for the education of both students and adults. Businesses are actively involved in school developments.

- Schools are only judged as successful if all students have the skills required to work within, and adapt to, a rapidly changing employment, social and economic climate.

- Formal education institutions are subject to 'market forces' bounded by democratically established forums.

The tension between teacher-centredness and learner-centredness is here apparently resolved. The learner is at the centre of the process, but what is to be learned and how it is to be learned are socially and democratically determined by communities, businesses, learners and teachers in response to the needs of the wider society. Viewed from one perspective, this situation might re-create the schools, colleges and curriculum approaches of the twentieth century; viewed from another – access to learning 24 hours a day, based on the student's capability and interest, facilitated by ICT and the Internet – something very new might be created.

Activity

Exploring the learning environment

In response to the previous reading, you tried to identify which approaches to learning and teaching were in operation at your school or college. Considering one of the approaches described above, imagine yourself observing a learning and teaching experience at your institution. What features of the learning environment would you identify as characteristic of the approach you have chosen?

❏ Our comments

There is not the space here to suggest a long list of features for each approach, and some features would appear in more than one list. However, your list might have included the following:

1. *Teacher-centred approach*
   Desks facing the front.
   Class listening and responding to the teacher.

2. *Learner-centred approach*
   Class working in groups around the room, or dispersed within – or outside – the building.
   Members of the learner group working on different tasks.

3. *Partnership approach*
   Resources provided by both teacher and learners.
   Learners and teacher consult each other about the learning process

4. *Inclusive approach*
   Different materials for different learners.
   Recognition and celebration of all kinds of achievement.

5. *Effectiveness approach*
   Class and teacher clear about the aims of the session.
   Plenty of purposeful feedback.

6. *Aspirational approach*
   You might not see a class at all!
   Learning via the Internet, with tutor support.

❏ Key learning points

- A range of analyses of learning styles exists, some of which have associated self-assessment materials: pupils and students can thus be encouraged to analyse their own learning style.

- Student and teacher awareness of individual differences in learning styles, and the 'learning conversations' that ensue when analyses take place, may be of more value than attempts to incorporate a particular theory of learning styles into teaching strategies.

- In Western cultures, adopting a range of teaching styles would appear to be beneficial to individual learners.

- In other cultures, particularly in Confucian societies, the motivators for learning may come from other factors – features of national, community or home culture that strongly support learning – and learning may be less dependent upon particular teaching strategies.

- The educational culture within which the learning and teaching takes place affects the attitudes of both learners and teachers to the learning experience. Strategies for learning and teaching may therefore not transfer readily from one culture to another.

- For reasons that may be pragmatic, political or value driven, a school or college – or an individual teacher within it – may adopt teaching approaches that are broadly teacher centred, learner centred or based upon partnership.

- Inclusiveness, effectiveness and aspirational models can each provide useful frameworks for school and college developments in learning and teaching.

Managing the learning environment

From considering the activities of learning and teaching themselves, we turn to consider the environment in which these activities take place. From an Australian perspective, Beare (1997) writes about features of school life that might usefully be 'left behind' if we were redesigning the process of education. Features of the learning environment that are listed include:

- Egg-crate classrooms and long corridors
- The division of the school day into standard slabs of time
- Parcelling of human knowledge into predetermined boxes called 'subjects'
- The assumption that learning takes place in a place called 'school'
- The artificial walls which separate school from home and community (adapted from Beare, 1997, pp. 2–4).

Activity

Wish list for future learning

What features of the learning environment would you choose to leave behind in redesigning your school or college to meet future needs? What features are you and your colleagues attempting to change already? What is the rationale behind your choice? How does it link with the changes in pedagogy we discussed in Chapter 1?

❏ Our comments

Your list may be similar to that of Beare and show a concern about the seemingly arbitrary 'compartmentalisation' of learning. You may be more concerned about the way learning is managed: who takes responsibility for what (and why?), or about the nature of the incoming students or the skills and approaches of the staff, or even about whether we need colleges and schools at all. Your list will probably take account of changes that are already starting to take effect, or are just appearing on the horizon, due to prevailing changes in pedagogy. Whatever your approach, you will have started to consider the environments in which learning takes place.

Many features of Beare's list are to do with boundaries and compartmentalisation – of the classroom, of the school day, of human knowledge. Where knowledge and experience can be obtained in the home, in the community, in the workplace, through people other than teachers, through 'hands-on' activities or through virtual environments, how relevant are the physical constraints of the school or college environment to today's learners?

In the sections below we shall consider the management of learning environments within the school and college then turn our thinking to learning beyond the classroom.

Classroom climate

Both national and international studies have identified 'classroom climate' as an important factor in student achievement. Wang *et al.* (1997), in their meta-analysis of learning influences, identified classroom climate as one of the most important features impacting upon student achievement. Likewise, an OECD study in 1994 of teaching in 11 countries concluded that creating a positive climate in the classroom was a key indicator of quality in teaching. According to such writers as Freiberg and Stein (1999) and Creemers and Reezigt (1999), the classroom climate is the mood or atmosphere created by:

- The layout of the learning environment
- The spoken and unspoken rules in operation
- The types of interaction between teacher and students.

The first element – the layout of the learning environment – will be discussed below in the section 'The physical learning environment'. The other two elements – the spoken and unspoken rules and the type of interaction between teacher and students – are influenced both by the teaching strategies adopted, which were discussed in the previous section, and by teacher expectations, which are discussed below.

❑ *Positive influences on classroom climate*

The Hay McBer report (DfEE, 2000) into teacher effectiveness also links the 'climate' of the classroom to the *expertise of the teacher* within it. The report identifies three main factors that contribute to effective teaching: professional characteristics, teaching skills and classroom climate. The evidence collected indicates that, taken together, these three factors predict well over 30% of the variance in pupil progress:

> So we show that teachers really do make a difference. Within their classrooms, effective teachers create learning environments which foster pupil progress by deploying their teaching skills as well as a wide range of professional characteristics. Outstanding teachers create an excellent classroom climate and achieve superior pupil progress largely by displaying more professional characteristics at higher levels of sophistication within a very structured learning environment (DfEE, 2000, para. 1.1.9).

Research from Israel offers a vivid example of the effectiveness of learning and teaching in individual classrooms. Yair (1997) reports on research carried out across the Jerusalem primary school sector that analysed the results of over 19,000 children in school grades 2–6 throughout the city for standardised tests in reading and mathematics. As might be expected, results were lower for children whose parents had low educational achievements or low socioeconomic status; there was a tendency for girls to achieve higher reading scores than boys, whilst boys scored higher, on average, in mathematics. Allowing statistically for these factors, results from different schools – and different classroom teachers – were then analysed. The startling outcome was that the variation in results of individual classes within schools was greater than that between schools. The finding was – to quote the title of the research paper – 'classrooms matter'. In primary schools where single teachers teach most of the school curriculum to their particular class, class teachers and the classroom climate they create have a significant influence on the effectiveness of learning.

One key to establishing a purposeful classroom climate is the *discourse* that takes place there. In a seminal work on culture and pedagogy, Alexander (2001, p. 5) emphasises the power of language in shaping what is distinctive about learning and teaching. The types of interaction between teacher and students is strongly characterised by the language used: 'It is in the discourse between teacher and pupils that education is done, or fails to be done' (Edwards and Mercer, 1981, p. 101). The language used is based upon the underlying culture: 'the web of inherited ideas and values, habits and customs, institutions and world views which make one country, one region, or one group, distinct from another' (Alexander, 2001, p. 5).

❑ *Teacher expectations*

Alexander's 'web of inherited ideas and values' may well have a strong influence on teacher expectations of individual students or of student groups, which is the aspect of classroom climate to which we turn next. Teacher expectations influence student achievement. For example, seminal research in the 1960s by Rosenthal and Jacobson revealed a 'Pygmalion effect' at work in the classroom. In a controlled experiment at the beginning of the year, teachers were given a list of students who were expected to do well. In this case, the judgement was arbitrary: these students had not displayed any particular 'promise'. Yet they did well, gaining more points in IQ scores and higher reading grades than did the control students. The teachers also rated the experimental group as having more intellectual curiosity than the control group (Rosenthal and Jacobson, 1968). The teachers would appear to have been influenced by the original 'judgement', and treated the 'promising' students more positively.

Negative expectations can be attached to students of a certain gender, social or ethnic group, or even in extreme cases to whole institutions: 'Well, what do you expect from young people around here?' In these cases, an existing social disadvantage becomes replicated and intensified within the learning arena. A vivid example from the UK context of the complex inter-relationship of factors that may create low expectations is offered by MacBeath (1999, p. 22):

> The experience of a low attaining English middle class girl with parents of Indian background needs to be probed with a more textured understanding of peer group affiliation, racial and sexual harassment, ascribed roles, sub-cultural tensions and parental and teacher expectations. High achieving Afro-Caribbean boys may experience particularly acute difficulties in adjusting to the different expectations of peers, teachers, their families and the group identity which defines them as not only a threat to the authority of teachers but to that of the police and others in positions of power.

You may be able to substitute examples from your own teaching context of students upon whom there are strong, conflicting, expectations. Whether teachers will be able to offer a 'textured understanding' of the situation will depend not only upon their own experience and skills, and the staff development they have received, but also upon the ways in which pupils and students are regarded at their institution.

❑ *Differential achievement*

As indicated in the above example, in the UK there has been concern in recent years about the achievement of certain minority ethnic groups, which in turn may have affected teacher expectations. Afro-Caribbean boys are of the greatest concern as they may be systematically underachieving, even in relation to working-class white pupils (Gillborn and Gipps, 1996, p. 22). This group is also the most likely of all ethnic groups to be permanently excluded from school (Croner, 2000). There is uneven evidence for the underachievement of Bangladeshi pupils but, in some areas, notably Tower Hamlets in London, achievement levels have been dramatically rising (Tower Hamlets LEA, 1994). On the other hand, Indian boys and girls have been achieving better than white pupils in some areas (Gaine and George, 1999, p. 109).

The underachieving children are considered to have inequality of access to learning: through the nature of the curriculum itself, through the style of classroom interaction, and even through the atmosphere in school corridors. Datta (1994) reported on measures aimed at improving the classroom climate for these students, which included cross-ethnic tutoring, with pupils from different ethnic backgrounds tutoring each other, and the use of more co-operative teaching methods. Pupils' respect for each other as individuals grew through this approach, and the 'at risk' tutees made both academic and social gains.

A further recent concern in the UK has been about the underachievement of boys in comparison to girls, investigated by Epstein (1998), among others. It is felt that recent approaches to learning and teaching, together with changing modes of assessment, have been less conducive to boys' learning styles than girls'. This, together with a prevailing culture of 'laddishness' – a macho disregard for learning – has been putting pressure on boys and girls alike. Experiments have been made with single-sex classes and changes in teaching styles to address the situation, which have largely resulted in an improvement in classroom climate and raised examination scores for both boys and girls. These attempts to re-engage boys with learning follow on from earlier concerns about girls' underachievement, particularly in maths and the sciences. In other countries, gendered patterns of achievement are likely to differ from those described here. An extreme example is the situation in some fundamentalist Islamic societies, where girls have no official access to education but, even in less extreme situations, the gender-based expectations of society, both of academic achievement and of potential adult roles, affect both teacher and student attitudes to learning.

❑ *Evaluating classroom climate*

Unfortunately, teachers sometimes have a more positive view of their classroom climate than do their students (Fraser, 1999). It is important, therefore, to seek out opinions in order to evaluate from other viewpoints, and to act on the evaluation. Muijs and Reynolds (2001, p. 59) suggest that evaluation could be carried out through structured observation of teaching and through inviting formal feedback from students, parents and community members. They indicate a number of ways in which incoming, on-course and outgoing students can be asked to assess classroom climate. They suggest that young pupils, for whom a questionnaire would be inappropriate, can be asked to draw their classroom, or to draw what they think is important within it, in order to elicit their perceptions. Areas for improvement can be targeted, and the evaluation repeated to see if an effect has been made.

This approach to assessing college or school 'climate' can also be taken at a whole-institution level. Martinez and Munday (1998) analysed the 'likes and dislikes' of 9,000 UK further education students and correlated their replies against whether the respondents persisted in their studies or dropped out of college. Among the likes and dislikes, 'relationships with other students' and 'relationships with staff', followed by 'social environment' and 'learning environment' were identified as the most important positive features of college, correlating with students' persistence with their courses. When considering college environment and culture, therefore, the authors propose that students are likely to remain on their courses when they encounter contexts for purposeful socialisation and for collaborative approaches to learning, together with stimulating and interesting learning opportunities. Collaborative approaches to learning and stimulating learning opportunities normally result from successful staff/student and student/student relationships combined with a well designed physical environment in which the learning relationships can be purposefully enacted. Where students are also encouraged to evaluate the constituent features of their school or college 'climate', teachers and managers are enabled to identify and address areas of concern.

Activity

Learners at risk

There is concern in most countries about the factors influencing the performance of particular student groups – for example, black students in newly 'mixed' South African schools, Maoris and Pacific Islanders in New Zealand schools, Moslem girls in a range of countries. Consider here what groups of learners give cause for concern in your country. What factors underlie the problem? How can teachers create a 'classroom climate' to try to address it?

❑ Our comments

The learners at risk may come from a minority ethnic group: one that is indigenous or newly arrived or lacking in social status. They may come from a particular social class or religious group. They may be of a particular gender. The quotation earlier from MacBeath (1999) warns us that, for some students, a complex network of factors may be at work.

Classroom approaches based upon the *inclusive approach* described above would make a good starting point, although elements of the other approaches, for example the *effectiveness approach*, would be appropriate. What may first be needed is a staff development programme that seeks to examine the social and learning needs of those who may be at risk in your school or college, and helps staff to devise strategies together to ensure consistency of approach.

The physical learning environment

In 1987, Adam conducted a survey of secondary schools in London with recently arrived headteachers. On being asked about the first change they had made on arrival at the school, almost all cited a change in the physical environment. For these heads this was a tangible statement of their arrival. Interestingly, for many the change benefited staff rather than students: was this a way of 'winning over' the staff through a visible token of better things to come? Deal (1988), when writing about features that contribute to institutional culture, cites 'buildings and facades' as visible signs of a predominating culture. Making changes to the building, therefore, may be making statements about a change in culture. It also marks an improvement in the 'physical capital' of the school (Caldwell and Spinks, 1992) and may have both practical and motivational benefits.

👁 *Reading*

Please read the chapter 'Managing the learning environment' by Ann Briggs, Chapter 11 in Middlewood, D. and Burton, N. (2001) *Managing the Curriculum*.

Here our attention is largely directed to the physical aspects of the 'climate conducive to learning'. How does the physical environment of your school or college classroom encourage learning, and in what ways does it reflect the culture of the institution?

❑ Our comments

In some institutions, resources are so scarce it is difficult to do much to enhance the physical environment. However, if your institution is above 'subsistence' funding, you may have identified such things as the type, ease of use and arrangement of classroom furniture; the ease of accessibility of ICT equipment; the lightness, ambient temperature and 'airiness' of the room itself; the display of student work and use of stimulating material around the classroom to catch the eye and engage the mind. These features may indicate cultures where students' physical needs are respected, their minds are stimulated and their achievements celebrated.

Your school or college may have inherited Beare's (1997) 'egg-crate' classrooms – features that can carry the connotation of regimented learning. You may work in a school that is too 'open plan' for present learning and teaching needs. Your college buildings may be so large and forbidding that less confident students fail to enrol or to engage with learning. The buildings may not be accessible for students who have difficulties with mobility or have impaired vision. The following section considers ways in which these situations might be addressed.

First, an audit can be carried out on the existing buildings, noting such features as potential health and safety hazards, size and configuration of teaching rooms, proximity of resource areas and support staff to teaching areas, flexibility and ease of use of furniture and classroom equipment, usefulness and accessibility of communal areas such as libraries and assembly halls, accessibility around the site for students with disabilities, state of internal and external repair and decoration, attractiveness and usability of outside areas. (This list is not exhaustive.) The following generic audit questions can be posed:

1. Where are we now? (assessment)

2. Where would we like to be in the future? (planning)

3. How best can we move in that direction? (implementation)

4. How do we evaluate the changes we are making? (evaluation) (Stoll and Fink, 1996, p. 17).

It is unlikely a school or college would have the resources to address all the features of the building and its site as suggested above. If no audit had been recently carried out, a 'broad brush' attempt to evaluate a large number of features under stage 1 (assessment) would be advisable in order to facilitate strategic planning. A decision would then be made to address only a small number of features through stages 2, 3 and 4, depending on the resources available. Selection of the features might be dictated by health and safety issues but, once those have been addressed, decisions are likely to be linked to the college's or school's strategic plan and to the ways in which it wishes to alter or reinforce its approaches to learning.

Level of resource is an issue, but costs need not be prohibitive. To take a simplistic example, a rural primary school in a developing country might need to spend its resources one year on mending holes in the roof, but might also wish (stage 2) to involve students more in each others' learning. Changing the configuration of tables and chairs in the room to suit a new teaching style would be the stage-3 response, and any benefits to learning could be evaluated as stage 4. If there had been benefits, then available resources in future years could be used to strengthen this teaching approach.

Stage 1: The data collected in answer to the question 'Where are we now?' might be extensive and discouraging, but this stage is necessary in order to identify priorities for action. At the very least, the assessment process encourages staff – and students if they also are involved – to take a fresh look at the environment in which they work. This awareness may enable small improvements to occur serendipitously: if the staffroom is collectively seen to be too cluttered to provide a useful base for teachers, the clutter may suddenly disappear; if corridors are seen as gloomy and uninspiring, parents and friends of the school might volunteer to paint them: they can then be decorated with students' work. If students have identified the entrance hall or reception area as being drab or unwelcoming, they may offer to put up displays that will interest and attract the learning community and visitors alike.

Major priorities, especially those that involve funding, will be identified through the school or college plan. Improvements that address the aspirations identified on the plan – better accessibility for people with disabilities; increased use of ICT; improved sporting success; more independent student learning – will receive priority, and will probably need more detailed assessment.

Stage 2 of the planning process asks the question 'Where would we like to be in the future?' This involves quantifying the type of aspirations described above:

- Which areas of the building are to be accessible to people with what kinds of disabilities?
- How many students will need computers at any one time, where and for what purpose?

- Which sports do we want to promote, and what facilities do they need?
- Will the independent learning take place on or off the premises? In what subjects?
- What resources are needed?

Answers to questions such as these will probably need specialist investigation by the subject managers involved, and a good measure of cross-institution discussion to be stimulated – and resolved – by senior managers.

In all the examples given above, changes to the physical environment would probably be needed. An example of this kind of development in action is provided in the case study of Leasowes Community College in the chapter 'Managing the learning environment' you have just been reading. Following their research into different approaches to learning, the staff wanted a proportion of their teaching to take place in large, well resourced, subject-based learning environments. They therefore decided to pull down walls between classrooms and incorporate sections of corridors and cupboards in order to create the learning spaces they wanted. This development was carried out gradually, partly in response to available funding, but partly so each area created could benefit from the evaluation of the previous one established.

Posing the question 'Where would we like to be in the future?' often helps institutions to identify some facilities that will no longer be needed. For example, in many UK further education colleges, large spaces that have become underutilised, such as assembly halls and older-style gymnasia, have been taken out of their initial use and turned into multimedia learning resource centres, incorporating library and computing facilities. Creative imagination, combined with ingenuity – and an injection of cash – can enable new styles of learning to be accommodated within old buildings.

Stage 3 – implementation – can be the most creative and dynamic stage of the planning process, as success at this stage can motivate staff and students to attempt further improvements. The case study of Booth Lower School in the chapter 'Managing the learning environment' is a good example of this. The school wanted to improve its library/computing area – and certainly achieved this – but the implementation process involved a chain of developments, all of which were beneficial to the school: a specialist area for learning support, a new teaching area for numeracy and literacy work, improved external play areas. Some of these were achieved simply by the staff being able to look at the school with 'new eyes' once the change process had started, and to identify improvements that could be made at little cost. As Fullan (1991, p. 90) notes: 'Improvement of practice is a continuous process of renewal.'

Even in a small primary school, there may be 'territorial' factors that can impede development. In a larger institution, these are likely to be even more pronounced. Murphy (1994, p. 52) writes vividly of territorial attitudes encountered in further and higher education: 'It is not uncommon for departments to regard a certain group of rooms for "their use" . . . Old plans are produced, "proving" the claim; and there are anecdotal tales of locks being changed to keep out "undesirable" members of the institution.' Conversely, development may be impeded because an area of the college does not seem to 'belong' to anyone, and staff are unwilling to suggest developments of areas they do not 'own'. Taking a whole-institution approach as suggested above can overcome this problem. In a case study by Coleman and Briggs (2000), a college learning resource centre was extended by expanding into space that had been formerly occupied by several administrative departments of the college; they in their turn were moved into spaces converted from former classrooms. This development therefore involved whole-college co-operative planning, which could not have been achieved within the conventional constraints of departmental 'ownership'.

Stage 4: 'How do we evaluate the changes we are making?' One simple way is to ask the pupils, students or staff what their perceptions are. Another is to assess improvements in achievement: did the college succeed better at the sports it had identified and provided for? Did children succeed in learning through the computer-based materials? Did the encouragement of independent learning correlate with improved exam results? Once the decision has been made to alter the learning environment, the money spent and the effort put into achieving the change, it is tempting to accept the new status quo. However, evaluation of recent developments can not only lead to necessary adjustments being made to the new provision but it can also lead to more informed decision-making for future developments.

Activity

Auditing the built environment

Choose one aspect or physical area of your school or college buildings and grounds. Think through the four audit questions in relation to the 'built environment': the building, external area, classroom, corridor, etc., and in relation to the equipment within your chosen area. Once you have outline answers to the audit questions, consider the following:

- Whom would I consult if I wanted to achieve this?
- Why might they agree to my ideas?
- What funding would we need?
- How might we achieve the task?

❏ Our comments

If you are a senior member of staff at your institution, you will be planning provision for your pupils and students on a regular basis. Perhaps the exercise has helped you identify an area you might otherwise not have considered. If planning of this kind is not normally part of your role, share your thoughts with others at your school or college. Often it is those who are close to a situation – needing a more specialist classroom, needing improvements to an external play area – who come up with the best ideas. If you get a positive response to your ideas, think how you can take your proposal further.

Learning beyond the classroom

In the chapter 'Managing the learning environment', you read about initiatives that involve learning outside the school or college boundaries. In this context it can sometimes be difficult to see where the boundaries are. In the UK, trainees may be employed and receiving training in the workplace, under audit and assessment schemes provided by a local college; in China, students may be involved in work/study schemes attached to their school, involving manufacture or agriculture. In these cases the learning environment encompasses both contexts, and school/college/workplace boundaries are indistinct.

Figure 2.3 attempts a representation of the 'nested' learning environments in which a school or college may be operating. In each case, managers and teachers may be working to bring the community influences into the institution, to take the learners 'out' to experience aspects of their community and environment as a learning experience, or the learning environment might encompass both institution and community on a more or less permanent basis.

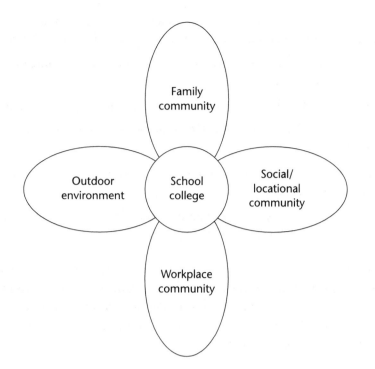

Figure 2.3 Learning beyond the classroom – 'nested' learning environments

❏ *Family community*

This 'nest' is strongest at the earliest stages of learning and in many cases where learners have learning difficulties or disabilities. Parents shape their children's preschool learning experiences, either by helping their children learn through home experiences or in some communities through young children accompanying a parent to work. Woodhead (1999, p. 118) reports that 'Comparing mother-child dyads in India, Guatemala, Turkey and the USA, Rogoff et al (1993) found that collaboration in joint activity was universal'. This activity was defined by Woodhead (1998, p.118) as 'Purposeful adult activity designed to initiate young children into socially valued skills'.

Parents, especially mothers, often take part in preschool learning activities in playgroups and nurseries. In many countries the child's move to formal education is marked by a home visit from a teacher or liaison worker from the school. Primary school parents are encouraged to attend sports days, concerts and religious ceremonies held at the school and to keep in regular contact with the child's teacher. Yet there are practical problems in creating a 'learning link' between school and home:

> It is easier for parents *not* to liaise with schools than it is to do so. There are quite practical deterrents. For instance, it is usually assumed that to have contact, parents must go to teachers, not vice versa . . . If contact is during school hours, some parents, especially fathers, may be prevented by work commitments . . . Cultural differences, including language problems, can also deter some . . . Further, schools are sometimes cold, unwelcoming places and parents may retain distressing memories of their own schooldays (Macbeth, 1993, p. 197).

Yet children continue to learn informally within their families, with or without liaison with the school. The family influences may be beneficial: instilling an enthusiasm or a respect for learning, which motivates the child to succeed, or they may be negative, perhaps reflecting and reinforcing disenchantment with education brought about by the parents' childhood learning experiences. This means schools may be working hard to build bridges to the family communities whilst at the same time attempting to separate the school from any negative features of family life. At its most positive, the 'family community nest' would involve the following activities (the list is adapted from Epstein, 1995, by Stoll and Fink, 1996, p. 136):

1. Parenting – helping each home to create an environment which supports learning, such as the school providing advice on supportive learning practices which can be carried out at home.

2. Communicating – developing two-way, jargon-free, meaningful communications about school programmes, practices and pupil progress.

3. Volunteering – recruiting and supporting parental and community help in the school.

4. Learning at home – helping parents to support their children's homework, and other curriculum and school-related activities.

5. Decision-making – including parents in meaningful school decisions as well as encouraging parental leadership on important school issues.

6. Collaboration with the community – identifying and integrating appropriate resources and services from the community to support the family and the pupils.

As you can see, this list includes links outwards from school to home: helping parents to support students at home; links inwards from home to school; recruiting parental help in the school; and school/parent liaison where both are involved in joint decision-making and leadership. If you work in a phase of education where family links are important, you might like to consider examples from your own institution for all three types of involvement.

❏ *Social/locational community*

This 'nest' is likely to be strong for all learners, as their learning, and attitudes to it, are shaped by the values of the community in which they are located. Communities with strong religious affiliations or strong locational identities – rural communities, inner-city areas – often have a pervasive culture with which the learner may identify or, in later years, reject. However strongly directional or diverse the culture is, it provides the context within which the learners attempt to make sense of their learning.

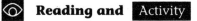 **Reading and** Activity

Read again the section 'Learning beyond the classroom' – pages 179–81 in the chapter 'Managing the learning environment' by Ann Briggs, Chapter 11 in Middlewood, D. and Burton, N. (2001) *Managing the Curriculum*.

Some of the examples given here are of activities that help students to learn through greater involvement in community life. List for yourself the activities with which your school or college students are involved and which enable them to learn through contact with the local community. Do not include work experience as we shall consider this in the next section.

- Are the activities you have listed optional, or are they built into the curriculum?
- Who organises them: the student, the class teacher or a school or college manager?
- What are the benefits to the student?
- What are the constraints in setting them up?

❏ **Our comments**

The constraints may be so great you have nothing on your list at all. If that is the case, this might be a matter worth addressing once you have considered the potential benefits of having such activities. If you have a list, its contents will vary according to the phase of education you are involved in and the country in which you live, but may include:

- Voluntary work with the young, the sick or the elderly
- Local environmental projects
- Surveys and studies of the local community as a part of the curriculum
- Visits by members of the community to the school or college to give talks, mentor students, lead activities or give performances
- Taking part in local religious observance
- Taking part in community sporting, theatrical or cultural activities.

Once more the possibilities include 'outward' movement of students, 'inward' importing of community members as a resource and joint undertakings indicating partnership. All three types of activity help the learners to make sense – and use – of their learning within their community setting.

Work with young people described by Bentley (1998) includes projects set up in socially deprived areas of the UK that aim to counter the negative effects of the local environment through positive engagement with beneficial aspects of it. He comments (1998, p. 89) that:

> Fighting against it [culture], especially in an age when global media are ever more accessible and influential, is fruitless. Rather than block it out, effective educators allow it to penetrate to the core of the learning process, and encourage the development of young people who are equipped to understand, judge and shape it, rather than being passive recipients of whatever comes their way.

Bentley describes how, through engagement in sport, popular music, the performing arts and ICT projects, young people are helped to build a sense of personal identity and confidence in themselves, which prepares them for positive experiences in adult life. For some of the most disaffected learners, who have stopped attending school, this is their primary learning experience.

Other projects bring the community into the school. Just as parents may be involved in hearing children read, or grandparents may be invited to talk about their early lives as 'living history' lessons, other community members may be involved as mentors, sports coaches or in running specialist sessions on aspects of health or the public services. Sometimes the influence of these links from 'beyond the school walls' can have a powerful effect. Provided the 'visitors' can relate to the learning context, they may carry great currency and credibility with the young people in bringing specialist knowledge and skills to the classroom.

In an article about education in post-Pinochet Chile, Aedo-Richmond and Richmond (1999, p. 206) note the presence of 'community monitors, typically local young people who offered extra assistance and personal attention to third and fourth grade students through after-school workshops'. Improvement in academic standards and levels of motivation have similarly been brought about in UK schools by mentoring schemes such as the one described by Bentley (1998, p. 92), which involved, among others, 'a corporate financier from the City of London sitting down to read once a week with an impoverished Bangladeshi child', and the Society of Innovators project scheme in Sweden, also described by Bentley (1998, p. 94), aimed at tackling youth unemployment in underpopulated rural areas. In a three-way partnership, young people create their own project, each guided by a slightly older peer mentor, with an adult monitor responsible for supporting the older peer. In all the examples given here, the benefit is not only to the child or young person but to the monitors and mentors themselves in increasing, for example, their social skills, personal confidence and knowledge of young people within their community.

Sometimes school and community agencies work together for the benefit of the students. For example, special schools in most Western contexts enlist the services of a wide range of professionals in order to provide a comprehensive service for their students. Thus, a school for students with severe or profound learning difficulties would, in addition to its teachers and support staff, need to draw on expertise from doctors, nurses, physiotherapists, occupational therapists, speech and language therapists, music therapists, educational psychologists, social workers and others. Such a multi- or interdisciplinary approach will, of course, be dependent on the resources available within that community and, therefore, provision is rarely equitable across regions or countries. In the school named in the literature as COSS, in Ontario, Leithwood *et al.* (1999) describe how a wide array of social services are provided by specialists within the school:

> Here, the need is so great that they bring the community services to the school. They have social services coming twice a week. They have a health nurse who comes in if kids are pregnant. We have a girl from the family health centre . . . Otherwise the kids have to go all the way down to [town] (teacher, quoted in Leithwood *et al.*, 1999, p. 95).

This focus on whole-community provision for students has led to a change in attitude in staff, from focusing on curriculum subjects to focusing on students:

> Once I began to realise that the world would probably still go on without . . . [my subject area], I began to look at it being more from the point of [view of] people rather than subject area. Here I began to realise that there was more of a people focus . . . (teacher, quoted in Leithwood *et al.*, 1999, p. 96).

Curricula that specifically aim to foster the development of awareness and involvement in the local and national community are to be found in a number of countries. Le Métais (1998, pp. 102–106), listing a range of curriculum aims from various countries, includes the following community-centred aspirations:

Australia – understanding and respect for cultural heritage; students to be enabled to act as active and informed citizens in a democratic Australian society.

Canada – to teach all young people something about common values and social behaviour and the intellectual and other traditions which support the common good in community, province and nation.

England and Wales – preparation for the opportunities, responsibilities and experiences of adult life.

Hungary – to prepare learners for life in a modern market economy, to prepare the country for full integration into Europe, to develop Hungary as a democracy.

Italy – preparation for adulthood and citizenship.

Korea – to promote patriotism and affection for others for the continuation of national independence as well as world peace.

New Zealand – to prepare learners to participate as active and informed citizens in a democratic society, within an international context.

USA – to teach learners to use their minds well, so that they may be prepared for responsible citizenship.

Given these are only extracts from the curricular aims of the nations concerned, a heavy responsibility is laid upon schools and colleges, which probably cannot be carried without the active involvement of the community beyond the school.

❏ *Workplace community*

The workplace community becomes increasingly important as students get older and education becomes more explicitly designed to prepare them for a working life. A UK survey in 1995 (Hillage *et al.*) found that 58% of primary schools and 92% of secondary schools had links with business: it can safely be assumed that the figure for further education colleges would be 100%, for reasons explained below. In schools, the first outward links into the workplace may take the form of a period of work experience, either in the type of employment the student wishes to take up in later life or with any local employer to give the student a taste of working life. In the chapter 'Managing the learning environment' (Middlewood and Burton, 2001) mention is made of an Australian scheme described by Cumming and Carbine (1997). The strength of this scheme was that it was incorporated into the school curriculum so that the learning acquired in the workplace was acknowledged within the school. The participants were enabled to identify skills they had learned in the workplace and how the skills contributed to their learning goals.

The full benefits of workplace learning are possible when the student – the young person or adult – is studying within a chosen vocational area and is either based in a college or technical school that has strong links to local businesses, service areas or industry, or is based in a workplace that has strong links with college provision. Here the bulk of the learning may take place beyond the classroom – in fact, the trainee may never attend the college at all. The vocational skills are either learned in the workplace or refined and tested there, with the college providing assessment, routes to accreditation and, in many cases, theoretical input. In the UK, the skills to be assessed are prescribed and monitored by professional 'lead bodies' for the vocational area concerned.

Managing outward links to business and industry thus becomes a major role for managers in vocational education. Liaison with local employers has to be maintained to ensure a common understanding of provision for trainees, and the quality of the provision, both within the workplace and the college, has to be measured against industrial and professional standards. Lumby (2001b, p. 127), writing of the 'vocationalisation' of the curriculum and drawing both on her own research and that of Ainley and Bailey (1997), notes a tension between 'providing what the employer or potential employer wanted' and the needs of the individual student. Some curriculum managers in Lumby's survey 'agreed that the curriculum might be diminished by an overemphasis on vocational aspects' (2001b, p. 127), but there was a counter-view that 'the emphasis on vocational aspects was to the benefit of disaffected students'.

The vocational provision is sometimes established as a direct result of local employer needs. In an article about vocational education in Brazil, Gomes (1991) describes how a group of local employers, in an area where local training facilities were deficient and there was no possibility of state provision, set up their own technical school. They offered technical education from school fifth grade up to adult education and training, in a mixture of daytime and evening provision: 'The atmosphere in the school is one of energy and commitment. The school and its students are highly visible in the community, and are subject to continual evaluation by local businesses' (Gomez, 1991, p. 461).

For some students, the school or college is also the workplace. In the UK there is a strong tradition of land-based colleges, which are commercial agricultural, horticultural or forestry enterprises as well as being specialist educational institutions. In China, Fouts and Chan (1997) report on work-study enterprises in primary and secondary schools, involving school factories and farms and incorporating such vocational skills as word processing, mechanical drawing and bicycle maintenance. From 1957, work study was an official part of the national curriculum of China; since the end of the Cultural Revolution, some schemes have been disbanded but the concept and the practice remain an accepted part of the curriculum.

In some countries there is a tension between the school and the workplace community: where students and even children are working long hours in employment outside school, for their own or their families' financial benefit, college and school work – and even attendance itself – can suffer. The financial imperative can be so great the learning process is impeded.

The section that follows draws heavily upon the work of Fuller and Unwin (2002, pp. 112–14); it offers a useful set of models when considering how workplace learning is organised and experienced. We hope that models set out here may help you to analyse the process and practice of workplace learning with which your own institution is involved.

- *The transmission model* 'Skills and knowledge are passed on in a formal manner within a hierarchical framework, either in the workplace itself or in an off-the-job setting' (Fuller and Unwin, 2002). This model is based on clear demarcation of job roles and uniformity of practice. It also assumes a hierarchy of knowledge and power within the workplace that transfers to the learning situation.

- *The tacit skills model* This is a model of experiential learning, where tacit skills are passed on through informal learning processes. This is principally an individual activity, reliant on a learner-centred approach that encourages reflective learning. It may take place alongside more formal models of learning, and Eraut *et al.* (1998) consider it is integral to the work context where learning grows out of purposeful social interactions.

- *Communities of practice model* This model, attributed to Lave and Wenger (1991), combines elements of both the transmission and the tacit skills model: 'Learning here involves participation in socially situated practices, and is an activity which is historical and dialectical' (Fuller and Unwin, 2002). Here the learner, through both formal and informal methods of knowledge transmission, becomes accustomed to – or may struggle against – the prevailing community of practice within the workplace, and recognises its relationship to the community outside the workplace.

- *The outcomes-based or competence-based model* Here the outcomes of learning are detached from the learning process. Teacher trainers guide the learning process, and assessors – who may be the teachers and trainers themselves – assess the skills and knowledge gained against agreed competencies for the profession. Although this approach is deemed to focus upon the individual learner, there have been criticisms of this model for encouraging a 'tick box' approach to learning (Hodkinson and Issitt, 1995; Raggatt and Williams, 2000).

- *The activity theory model* As with the 'tacit skills' model, this model acknowledges that people learn from social interactions with their working colleagues; it proposes this learning can be further progressed though structured learning and teaching. The learning may not always be applied, or even fully understood, at the time of acquisition: 'People and organisations are all the time learning something that is not stable, nor even defined or understood ahead of time' (Engestrom, 2001, p. 137).

❑ Links between business and schools

Much of the discussion in this section so far has been concerned with learning *in* the workplace. The workplace community is also important when we consider links *between* the workplace and the school or college. In her chapter 'Working with employers and business' in Lumby and Foskett (1999), Coleman outlines the benefits to business and to schools and colleges of maintaining business links. The main points are outlined below but, for a fuller discussion, please read the whole chapter.

1. *Benefits to business* Links between business and industry on the one hand and schools and colleges on the other are seen by Coleman (1999, p. 166) as *mutually beneficial*. The educational establishment benefits from input from 'outside', whether in the form of resources or personal expertise. Industry and business can use the links to meet what they see as their concern for their local community and its environment, as well as enhancing the skills of its present – and potential future – workforce. In examining what might be considered as 'optional' links for business – i.e. those not directly concerned with training their own staff – surveys of UK businesses indicate that some go beyond the purely pragmatic in their involvement in education:

> The evidence . . . is that employers are primarily driven by motives wider than mere self-interest. Across the whole sample, respondents were more likely to signal their agreement with the statements that indicated some form of benevolent or, in particular, enlightened, self-interest motive for their involvement with education (Hillage *et al.*, 1995, pp. 13–14).

2. *Curricular benefits* Whilst the majority of business links are with secondary and post-compulsory establishments, there is some evidence of partnerships with primary schools, both through direct contact with pupils in school and through business placements for teachers. In the USA, for example, there are examples of collaboration between 'educators, health care providers, business people and communities to help give children a fighting chance of performing at high levels in school and becoming contributing members of society' (Green, 1993, p. 142).

In secondary and post-compulsory education, the 'desirable outcomes' identified by Marsden (1989, p. 26) are 'communication skills, economic and industrial awareness, technological capability, health education and a whole range of other skills and attitudes'. Warwick (1989, p. 21) sums up the various benefits of education–business links as follows:

Social – extending the students' knowledge of society to include industry and business

Economic – enhancing economic and industrial understanding, perhaps through enterprise education

Vocational – preparation for the world of work including careers education

Affective – learning 'through' industry rather than about it; the development of skills such as communication and team work through simulated activity

Pedagogic – drawing relevant examples to enliven the curriculum from local industry

Instrumental – passing on knowledge, experience and practical skills.

These benefits could be applied to links with any phase of education.

Finally in her chapter, Coleman (1999, pp. 169–72) considers specific examples of business–education links that have potential curricular benefits. These are as follows:

1. Enterprise education – Here students are involved in simulated activity which may include role-play, in order to replicate 'real-life' business situations, particularly decision-making. The emphasis is on experiential learning, with the teacher as facilitator.

2. Mentoring of students by industrialists – In mentoring schemes, under-achieving students are often targeted for one-to-one mentoring with volunteers from a business setting. Although to date there is little evidence of improved examination results, there are recorded benefits for the self-esteem and motivation of the students – and the mentors.

3. Placements of teachers and lecturers in industry – These schemes are mainly found in secondary and post-compulsory education. Their main purpose is to update the vocational skills and awareness of the vocational setting of the school or college teacher.

4. Work experience for students – This is the most frequently recognised link between business and education. The benefits are usually seen as both vocationally and personally developmental, although other curricular benefits are cited, for example: 'a means through which students could be assisted to explore their community and critically to examine various elements of society' (Watts, 1991, p. 49). As has been discussed above, if students are to learn from their work experience, it needs to be well integrated into their curriculum.

❏ *Outdoor environment*

Education takes place not only within the social, cultural and working environments of the learners but also – at all ages – within the physical outdoor environment. The land-based colleges mentioned earlier are a good example of learning within and through the physical environment as an integral part of the educational process. At the other end of the educational scale, primary school children are often encouraged to bring into school examples of the natural environment – for example plants, stones, shells or feathers – to illustrate current themes in their classroom learning.

Academic study of geographical, environmental and biological subjects often involves study trips, where students can be enabled to study the phenomenon 'in the field'. These can range from day excursions within the locality of the college or school to residential visits within the home country or overseas. Residential trips obviously have resource constraints, but where they are possible they also bring the benefit of a shared learning experience for staff and students: 'Release from the confines of the classroom, into the wider community, changed the attitude of the pupils and teachers, both to each other and to that which is to be learned' (Baddely, 1991, p. 103). In Denmark, residential experience is valued so highly there is provision for every child to go on a residential trip every year – an activity that involves many parents as helpers (Crombie White, 1997). This is only one part of a school provision that involves pupils, parents and teachers in social and cultural activities to foster the children's personal development.

Involvement in outdoor pursuits of various kinds can achieve the effect described above by Baddely. Such pursuits as walking, climbing and water sports create a new relationship between student and teacher: the teacher holds responsibility for the safe outcome of the event, but a mutual dependency is fostered in the group and individual students may show greater prowess at an activity than the teacher. Under these conditions, social skills are developed, relationships tested and hopefully strengthened, and individual physical skill promoted.

Activity

Learning beyond the classroom

Choose from the 'nested' environments that have been discussed above one which is particularly important in your phase of education. Why is this element of learning beyond the classroom so important for you? What are the positive and negative aspects or influences of the environment outside the classroom? How do you, as a manager or as a classroom teacher, keep the relationship with the external environment under control?

❏ Our comments

Each of the 'nested' environments surrounding the school or college contains within it vital resources and experiences for the young and adult learner alike. Making use of these external environments demands managerial skill and a sense of balance – balancing positive and negative influences from the external environment, balancing the needs of the learners and the collaborators, balancing the varying demands of the curriculum. As we have seen, the communities and environments external to the institution can benefit from the partnership: one task of the manager in setting up external liaison is to convince his or her collaborators of the genuine mutual benefits. Learning beyond the classroom involves large elements of risk, which must be properly assessed and managed; it also involves handing over control, sharing responsibility for education with members of the wider community.

❏ *Distance learning*

We cannot leave the concept of 'learning beyond the classroom' within a text such as this without discussing the management of distance learning. There is some tradition of distance learning in schools, particularly in remote areas such as the Australian Outback where physical access to school is difficult, but distance learning is mainly a learning mode undertaken by adults. Students may be separated from their college or university through geographical distance or by logistical factors such as restricted mobility or the constraints of employment. They may be learning within the workplace using materials provided by their employer – or by an accrediting institution – for acquiring particular skills. In many countries the practice of distance learning builds a strong historical tradition of independent learning for self-improvement.

Managing effective learning and teaching for distant students involves the same awareness of learners' needs as 'conventional' learning, and a strong infrastructure for addressing and meeting those needs. This infrastructure may include the following:

- Initial assessment of skills.
- Pre-entry counselling about how (or whether) the learner's needs can be met.
- On-course tutoring to support learning: by email, by telephone, by post, in some circumstances face to face.
- On-course support by administrators to clarify procedures.
- A range of learning materials, tailored to the course: paper-based and computer-based.
- Guidance as to how to 'navigate' the learning materials.
- Access to further learning resources via libraries and ICT.
- Access to other distant students for mutual support.
- Administrative systems to track student progress and achievement.
- Assessment systems in parity with face-to-face courses at the same level.

The virtual learning environment

Some of the distance learners considered above will be working through the use of ICT within a 'virtual learning environment'. Learners at the Midlands Further Education college described in Middlewood and Burton (2001) Chapter 11: 'Managing the learning environment' were following all or part of their courses through computer-based learning. Students remote from the college worked entirely from computer-based materials and had visual contact with their tutor through web-based cameras mounted on their computers. Within the college, managed learning environments were set up by tutors in order to 'free up' class time for such activities as group discussions of what had been learned, student presentations and one-to-one support. The managed learning environments included course material presented as web pages, with links to further resources, and discussion areas that could be monitored or led by tutors.

Are there common attributes of computer-based learning systems within schools and colleges? Dimmock (2000) reports on a synthesis of research by Hancock (1997), which identified six attributes of the 'Information Age' school:

- *Interactivity*: Schools where ICT is successfully integrated show high levels of interaction – between students, between students and staff, between students and their peers in other countries. Learners are skilled at accessing and handling information, and discuss their learning tasks with others.
- *Self-initiated learning*: 'Students take charge of their own learning.' They ask the questions, gather the data and analyse and interpret them in relation to the problem. This involves the use of higher-order skills.
- *Media and technology specialists as central participants*: Media and technology specialists are integral to the learning environment: they work with students and collaborate with staff, providing training where necessary.

- *Continuous evaluation*: Computer-based learning materials – both those in use and potential resources – are appropriately evaluated. Evaluations are shared with other users and with software developers.

- *A changed physical and human environment: a different classroom configuration and use of space:* The classroom space has been redesigned. 'Computers are central to the ambience of the classroom.' Co-operative learning, guided inquiry and thematic teaching are used as teacher strategies (adapted from Dimmock, 2000, pp. 173–75).

These factors emphasise the human side of learning through technology. Setting up systems that encourage *interactivity* with the tutor and with other students helps to maintain the all-important social aspects of learning. *Communication* between students, and between student and tutor, is reported by some researchers to be a 'richer' experience than in conventional classroom interaction: 'Electronically supported groups develop a richer communication structure with less hierarchical differentiation, broader participation and more fluctuating and situational leadership structures' (Bikson and Eveland, 1990, p. 285). In other words, the prevailing hierarchies of the classroom, with communication dominated by the tutor and the most confident students, can be overturned, with different students 'leading' the project and the discussion as the situation demands. The advantage for the less confident students is they can 'take time to ponder the various points made, and make contributions in their own time' (Laurillard, 1993, p. 168).

ICT-based learning can also enable students to take charge of their own learning to a level of *flexibility* that it is difficult to provide in classroom-based teaching; one important feature of this is choosing the time, place and pace of their learning. A further type of flexibility is provided through the range of possibilities for student engagement in *active learning*, as exemplified by Alden (1998, p. 4): 'They can interrupt the instruction whenever they wish, and reach out to the enormous wealth of information and resources available on the Web. They can produce products and participate in projects with other students and the instructor at the push of a button and receive individualised feedback.'

MacBeath and Mortimore (2001) claim that ICT development can foster a greater respect for the pupil voice, where pupils and students access learning resources well beyond those provided in the classroom and known to the teacher. A common phenomenon of the growth of ICT has been that pupils and students become more skilled than their tutors and acquire a tutoring, or even a staff developmental, role. This echoes the *changed physical and human environment* noted above.

Dimmock (2000), above, emphasises the role of *media and technology specialists as central participants.* Not only is this essential but they also need to work in close harmony with the teaching staff, an achievement that it is not always easy to secure. Betts and Smith (1998, p. 120) point out that ICT learning systems are often designed by technocrats who do not understand curriculum development, on behalf of academics whom they see as only semi-literate in ICT. Alden (1998, p. ix) warns us of a similar problem: 'Too often we become enamoured with the technological capabilities of our bright and shiny devices and ignore fundamental learning theory.' That theory has to adapt to the new medium: learning through ICT has to be approached and presented differently from learning in a classroom: 'If all we do is imitate a traditional classroom, then Web-based instruction will be a second-rate reproduction of the classroom experience' (Allen, 1998, p. x).

Students must be *appropriately prepared for the learning experience* they will encounter, both in terms of technical skill and confidence in learning through this route. Teachers must be *familiar with the learning routes* their students are to follow in order to offer appropriate guidance and support. Trentin (1999, p. 22) comments: 'Before directing students toward specific educational goals to utilizing the Internet, teachers must test first-hand the interaction opportunities the network offers.'

The importance of ICT-based initiatives – not least in the hoped-for impact on national economies – is underlined by the fact that in several countries they are the focus of national initiatives which include the central supply of (or funding for) hardware, the development and supply of software, the development of curricula both in ICT and using ICT, and the training of teachers. International agencies exist that have a role to share information and support software development, such as the Nordic Committee on Educational Software and Technology and the Centre for Educational Research and Innovation, supported by the OECD (McCormick, 1999).

Despite national and international support for ICT-based curricula, and the significant success of local initiatives, research by Betts and Smith (1998) and Alden (1998), among others, indicates there are often barriers to successful implementation. If too much emphasis is placed on the equipment and not enough on the people who are to use it, difficulties will be encountered. The key to success would appear to be in drawing together those with the technical knowledge and those who are leading the programmes of learning so that both can appreciate the learning routes the student will take and both will ensure the route is clearly mapped and that pedagogic and technical support are available:

> We have to realise that no medium, in or of itself, is likely to improve learning in a significant way when it is used to deliver instruction. Nor is it realistic to expect the Web, when it is used as a tool, to develop in students any unique skills. The key to promoting improved learning with the Web appears to lie in how effectively the medium is exploited in the learning and teaching situation (Owston, 1997, p. 29).

Achieving the necessary level of integration of people and systems demands a considerable process of change: to the vision of the school or college, to its management and operational systems, to the skill base of managers and teachers, to attitudes to the curriculum and to the learning process. It demands total commitment and a high level of skill in managing the change.

Activity

Using ICT resources

What level of use does your school or college make of virtual learning environments? What benefits have your learners gained from their use of ICT? Where would you like your institution to be in relation to ICT in five years' time? How will you get there? Whom will it involve? What do you see as the main constraints?

❑ Our comments

Your response will depend upon your starting point, but it is likely you will be planning for an increase in use of ICT in learning and may be unable to imagine what computer-based learning experiences will be available in five years' time. You may be wanting to develop ICT resources to support classroom teaching, to replace it or to transform its nature. It is likely your main constraints will be financial resources, staff attitudes and levels of expertise, the configuration of the building and access to technical expertise and ongoing support. Look in your local educational press to learn how other people overcame their constraints and 'got there'.

❑ **Key learning points**

- Classroom climate – the effects of the physical environment, the interaction between teacher and students and teacher expectations – is a vital element in influencing the learning process.

- An audit approach to managing the physical learning environment may produce change that is beneficial to learning.

- Much learning takes place – planned or unplanned – beyond the classroom. It is part of the role of the teacher to understand and manage interactions with the external environment to the benefit of the learner.

- The benefits of virtual learning lie in the wealth of learning experiences available to the learner, and the skills to be gained in accessing them. Overcoming logistical and attitudinal constraints demands a planned programme of change.

3. The management of learning

Introduction

In this chapter we turn to the roles and activities through which learning and teaching are managed. The roles and structures discussed in the first section vary from country to country, from phase to phase of education, and have different names in different institutions. The ways in which curriculum planning, monitoring and evaluation are carried out, and even the extent to which they are carried out, will likewise vary. Change manifests itself in different ways, and different 'local' strategies will need to be adopted to manage change successfully. We hope, nevertheless, you will engage with the underlying principles presented and analysed here and relate them usefully to your own experience.

Models of curriculum organisation and management

Curriculum management is crucial in ensuring that the conditions for successful learning are created and maintained. This is a dynamic process requiring attention at all levels of the organisation and throughout all phases of the education system. Whilst there are, obviously, differences in scope and complexity from the primary phase, through secondary and into the further education sector, there is also a common framework within which all educational institutions will operate. We have already examined some of the aspects of curriculum and learning and teaching that underpin the whole education system in the two previous chapters of this text. In this chapter we intend to consider the roles and activities through which learning and teaching are managed. This section concentrates on the structures for curriculum management that enable teaching and, most importantly, learning to take place.

It is important, in terms of the management of the curriculum, for the leader of the organisation (alone or collaboratively) to clarify key questions, whatever the actual age range in the school or college. For example:

- What is the school/college's key purpose?
- How is this purpose to be achieved?
- What are the significant issues to be addressed?

Approaches to these issues, in strategic terms, are addressed in the 'Leadership and Strategic Management' module. Whether the curriculum is defined as the total experience of the students at school or college or, more narrowly, in terms of what is taught or delivered, these questions remain central. Curriculum management therefore is partly generic management but it is also concerned with specific issues arising from consideration of purpose.

If the institution's key purpose is to ensure effective learning, the primary task in managing the curriculum is to influence or shape the environment within which this learning takes place. This would normally encompass the following:

- *What* is learned (and taught) (i.e. curriculum content).
- *The form* in which it is presented (i.e. curriculum design).
- *How* it is learned (and taught) (i.e. pedagogy, methodologies).
- *Creating the circumstances* under which these can be effectively achieved (i.e. developing an appropriate culture, utilising resources effectively, creating structures, etc.).
- *Assessing* how effective it is (i.e. evaluation).

Learning and teaching will be affected by a whole range of factors, including many that involve human resource management (e.g. staff recruitment and retention, staff and student attitudes, teacher performance and awareness of the needs and experiences of individual students). The management task can be seen as the establishment of a framework within which effective learning and teaching will take place. This framework may involve the following:

- *A culture* A general agreement on attitudes, views and values.
- *A structure* Whereby people and their tasks are related to each other.
- *A programme* Enabling the tasks of learning and teaching to be efficiently carried out through managing the availability of people, time and accommodation (timetable).
- *A plan* To give curriculum direction and progression.
- *A budget* To manage allocation of resources.

Some specific issues will, inevitably, be common to managing the curriculum, although individual issues may be major or minor considerations, depending on the context and situation. Duffy (1988, p. 112) suggests decisions will need to be made on:

- Subjects and courses
- Breadth and balance
- Differentiation, by age and/or ability

- Organization, by age and/or ability
- Learning and assessment objectives
- Testing and assessment techniques
- Monitoring and evaluation
- Resources – especially time, teaching and materials
- Equality of opportunity and treatment
- Special needs.

What those decisions are and, equally importantly, how they are taken, may be seen to be central to managing the curriculum and the headteacher/principal and curriculum managers at all levels are responsible for this. Lee and Walker (1997), building on the work of Whitaker (1993), suggest a whole-school, *holistic* approach to the curriculum will also require a paradigmatic shift in management and leadership. They offer (Lee and Walker, 1997, p. 103) the following comparison between the old and new paradigms, in the context of the Hong Kong maintained-school sector:

Old paradigm	New paradigm
Management	Leadership (all workers are managers)
Vertical ladder	Sideways (more open and participative decision-making structures)
Fixed roles	Flexible roles
Individual responsibility	Shared responsibility (teamwork)
Autocratic	Collaborative
Delivering expertise	Developing expertise (an effective system of staff appraisal and staff development)
Status	Stature (all participants are valued for their unique and special contribution)
Efficiency	Effectiveness
Control	Release (all members are able to commit their skills and energies to an organisation in a culture of encouragement and support)
Power	Empowerment (getting things done and supporting the people who do it).

Lee and Walker (1997) do point out that the shift to such a whole-school approach requires 'consider-able commitment, reflection, deliberation and collaboration between colleagues' and between staff and students but believe the effort involved will result in quality education.

We have already suggested in Chapter 1 that management structures are dependent on the context and staffing available, in the sense that larger will tend to mean more complex. As Burton *et al.* (2001, pp. 20–21) point out:

> Models of the curriculum cannot be developed or imposed in isolation from other influential factors. To an extent any model of the curriculum, as it exists in the educational establishment, will be a compromise between these various pressures; a reflection of reality and the vision that is being worked towards.

The influential factors referred to above are identified as pressures that may lead to a complication of the curriculum vision. The following tensions are described:

- Student-centred versus subject-focused
- Process versus content
- Classroom-led versus state-controlled
- Open-ended versus target-driven

⊚ *Reading*

Now read the full description of these pressures in Chapter 2 of Middlewood and Burton (2001), which you will find in the section entitled 'Characteristics of curriculum models' (pp. 20–27).

Whilst you are reading, try to determine which pressures exert the greatest influence on your own institution and how they have influenced the management of learning and teaching.

❑ Our comments

An important point made by Burton is that the more influences the curriculum has to satisfy, the more complicated will be the curricular vision. Although a mixture of approaches is usual in schools and colleges, you may need to ask how much can be incorporated before the resulting tension proves unmanageable.

The pressures on your own institution may be due to a number of factors, including the age range taught (learner centred approaches are traditionally seen in primary classrooms, for example) or to national directives about content or time allocations for subjects. Assessment is a key factor in shaping the curriculum, particularly where examination results are seen as the main indicator of success.

The management systems associated with a learner-centred school have been examined by Wagner (2000) in her case study of a modified Montessori school in Toronto. She identifies three key elements of the system that are referred to as *primary*, *enabling* and *supporting*. The interdependencies and relationships between these key elements are shown in Figure 3.1. The starting point (input) is the 'needs, preferences and interests of the student', and an explicit, cognitive-orientated learning and teaching technology (the Montessori method) forms the basis of the system. Perhaps surprisingly, this model is not democratic in nature; Wagner (ibid., p. 385) explains that:

> Throughout the system development, implementation, and evaluation processes, there is a clear and preferred separation between inputters (teachers, students, and parents) and decision-makers (directors) with respect to school management. Success is largely attributed to a non-consensual yet highly involving decision-making approach. As well, the directors consciously hire the values *and* the skills in resourcing the school, enabling relationships and personal communication to take precedence over pieces of wordy and detailed stand-alone documentation of management system elements.

Wagner also asks some pertinent questions in respect of her findings. She wonders whether the 'tightly integrated, minimally documented and highly focused' management system in place was, in fact, a function of the smallness of the school and asks whether the patterns that emerged from a primary and elementary setting would be apparent in middle and high-school learner-centred settings.

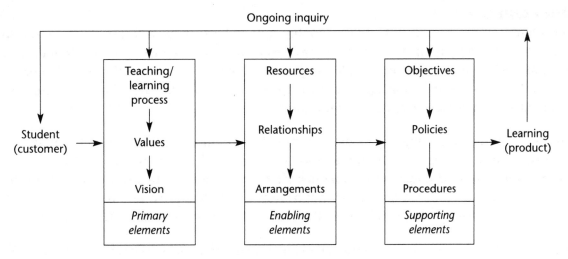

Figure 3.1 Management system design for a learner-centred school: a model
Source: Wagner (2000, p. 385)

Whatever system or structure is in place in a school or college, there is no doubt this is a necessary component of the effective management of learning and teaching. Mullins' description of organisational structure, quoted in Blandford (1997, p. 44) makes clear what it is and why it is needed:

> Structure is the pattern of relationships among positions in the organisation and among members of the organisation. The purpose of structure is the division of work among members of the organisation and the co-ordination of their activities so they are directed towards achieving the goals and objectives of the organisation. The structure defines tasks and responsibility, work roles and relationships, and channels of communication.

Before going on to look at some school and college structures, please complete the following activity, which asks you to look at your own organisation.

Activity

Structures for managing the curriculum

Think about your own school or college and try to define the structures that support management of the curriculum. Once you are clear about the main features, see if you can represent this in diagrammatic form to show the model for your organisation. You will need to consider who is involved and what their respective roles are.

If your school or college already has a published model, you may wish to reflect on how useful this is:

- Does everyone understand how it works?
- Does it reflect accurately what actually happens?
- Is it an effective way of managing?
- How could you improve it?

❑ **Our comments**

If you attempted the first activity, you probably found the task more complex than you at first thought. It is relatively simple to identify the key people and discrete tasks involved in managing the curriculum, such as timetabling or co-ordinating a subject area. However, difficulties often arise when you try to show the inter-relationships and interdependencies at work, particularly for cross-curricular responsibilities such as assessment or pastoral support.

If you were considering an existing model, you may have found some responsibilities have changed over time or that new roles have been identified since the model was first designed. Subjects and/or departments may have changed, with some merged or dropped altogether and new ones introduced. In extreme cases, the published model may not bear much relation to current reality, either because a radical update is urgently needed or because the model was never a very good fit anyway!

Where you felt improvements were necessary, these may be linked to internal or external factors that militate against change. Ownership of curricular initiatives is an important factor here and teachers have been known to subvert imposed initiatives which, they feel, do not offer a good fit (an internal factor). Lack of funding to ensure essential resources are in place (an external factor) would also block improvements.

The models in Figures 3.2–3.4 show traditional organisational structures for the primary, secondary and further education sectors, which are characterised by a hierarchical design in which roles and responsibilities are rigidly delineated.

We have already noted there is a need for flexibility in defining organisational structures. The three models illustrated can be seen to be rather lacking in the flexibility required to respond to a rapidly changing context. Schools and colleges will, therefore, adapt their structures accordingly. As a result, you may find the models presented do not match your own structure, either in part or entirely. Look again at the model you produced for the activity above and compare this with the traditional models we have present here: what are the similarities/differences between the two? You may find schools are starting to adopt a more collegial approach to managing the curriculum, with more emphasis placed on cross-curricular links and whole-school initiatives such as literacy development across all subjects. In FE colleges, a more complex, matrix structure (Fidler, 1997) would take account of 'dual authority relationships' and appears to offer more adaptability to change. In special schools, a combination of models may be most suitable to take account of a small organisation with complex structural relationships, which encompasses increased input from outside agencies (multidisciplinary models).

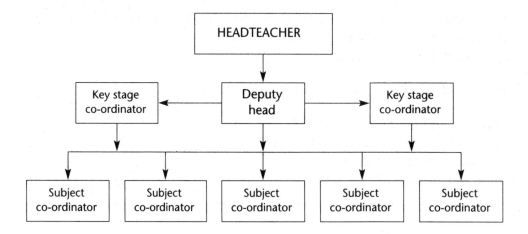

Figure 3.2 Primary school management – flat model
Source: Adapted from Blandford (1997)

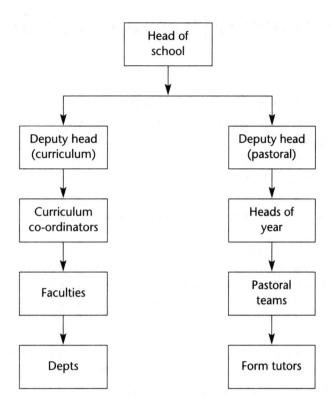

Figure 3.3 Secondary school management – parallel structures

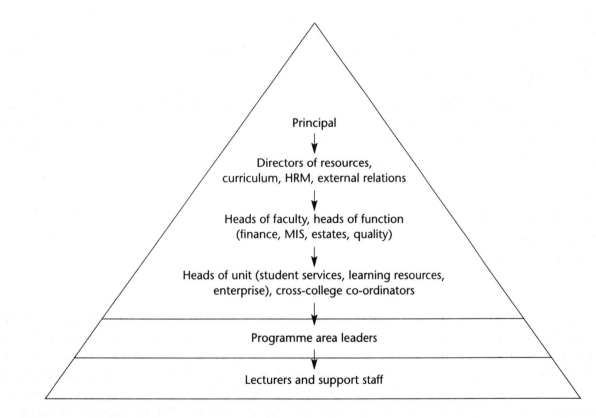

Figure 3.4 Simplified hierarchical pyramid structure – FE colleges
Source: Lumby (2001b, p. 90)

Roles and responsibilities in managing the curriculum

The core mission and values of a school or college provide a coherent framework within which the competing tensions of various stakeholder groups in the organisation might be resolved and harnessed in the pursuit of legitimate common concerns. Mission and values, as we have discussed in Chapter 1, provide an essential benchmark against which curriculum intentions and practice might be tested. A key objective of curriculum management, then, might be considered to be the establishment of an agenda for learning and teaching that moves beyond the mere transmission of a body of knowledge and skills and provides staff and students with a meaningful context for the development of those values:

> Education is not a value-free commodity . . . It is a social process and a learning process in which the teacher, the learner and those close to the process (parents and professionals) have to interpret and adapt the overall learning goals into the activities that are to be found in the school and the classroom. The constant need to work the curriculum through is as important for the teacher in making sense of what has to be taught as it is for the child in learning it (Goddard and Clinton, 1994, p. 57).

As you will know from your own experience, in some schools and colleges, curriculum managers will endeavour to find the time and space for colleagues to 'work the curriculum through'; in others, the curriculum will be accepted as given, particularly if it has been externally prescribed. In some communities, the prescribed curriculum will appear directly relevant to the learning needs of pupils or students; in others, not. In some sectors of education (for example, nursery or special school) teachers will feel able to exercise considerable discretion in what they offer to children; in others, such as upper secondary or further education, the curriculum may appear to have been closely defined by outsiders. In England, with the imposition of the National Curriculum, this may be the case for all sectors. Yet, as we have already discussed, effective learning needs to be relevant and responsive to students' needs, leading to a 'personalising' of the curriculum by schools or individual teachers.

In this section we will explore the roles and responsibilities of curriculum managers at different levels of the organisation. Our view is that everyone who has a responsibility for learning and teaching, including the students themselves, has a role in curriculum management. For the purposes of this discussion, we have categorised the key groups as:

- Senior management
- Middle management
- Classroom teacher
- Learning support
- Student.

There is a basic tension in management structures in any organisation. This concerns the balance between *differentiation* (i.e. the specialised roles and responsibilities accorded to individuals and groups) and *integration* (i.e. the need to co-ordinate the work of those individuals and groups so that different parts of the organisation work to common agendas) (O'Neill, 1994). It is not difficult to apply these tensions to autonomous schools and colleges. Traditionally, schools and colleges have operated on the basis of considerable differentiation; they have employed hierarchical management structures, they have often distinguished between academic and pastoral areas of the curriculum and advocated a clear distinction between the roles of teacher, student and support staff. More recently, the external pressures on schools and colleges from national initiatives and local delegation, from technological advances and the move towards globalisation, have all played a part in prompting considerable changes, many of which have created particular pressures on traditional management structures and arrangements for the organisation and delivery of the curriculum. Such developments create new imperatives for curriculum managers in schools and colleges:

1. Curriculum planning, development, delivery and assessment are no longer the preserve of individual classroom practitioners. Effective curriculum coverage demands collaborative planning and integrated approaches to curriculum delivery.

2. The development of complex curricula and the consequent fragmentation of traditional subject divisions create pressures for institution-wide policies on issues as diverse as assessment, record-keeping, basic skills, student support, the sharing of diagnostic information and independent learning. Individual curriculum managers are thereby under greater pressure to help define and then conform to whole-school or college policy.

3. External accountability pressures and the need to ensure complete curriculum coverage reinforce the need to observe classroom practice and offer constructive feedback on what has been observed.

How, then, should the allocation of responsibilities for managing the whole curriculum, including learning and teaching, be decided? All teaching jobs involve some management; this may be managing people or resources or learning activities at various levels of complexity. A good starting point for our discussion is the definition of management in its broadest sense, provided by Everard and Morris (1996, p. 4):

(1) Setting direction, aims and objectives;

(2) Planning how progress will be made or a goal achieved;

(3) Organising available resources (people, time, materials) so that the goal can be economically achieved in the planned way;

(4) Controlling the process (i.e. measuring achievement against the plan and taking corrective action where appropriate); and

(5) Setting and improving organisational standards.

By reference to the above definition, we would now like you to try the following activity, which asks you to apply the principles to the five management roles we identified, using the chart provided below. Please complete the activity before reading our comments, which follow it.

❏ Our comments

You will have found this activity easier to complete for some categories than for others, although it should be possible to identify management responsibilities for each principle across *all* categories. The student role may be the most difficult, particularly in the case of younger children or students with learning difficulties. However, if we accept that students should be encouraged to take on responsibility for their own learning, then some aspects will apply, albeit at possibly restricted levels.

In deciding how each level of management is reflected in practice, you may have felt some roles and responsibilities are fairly nominal; in other words, people may hold titles that confer no power for decision-making, or expectations may be unrealistic at that level of responsibility. For example, it may be quite appropriate to say to a student about to embark on a vocational course that it is his or her responsibility to plan how he or she will make progress in his or her studies; it would be totally unrealistic to expect a nursery child to do the same, without adult support and direction.

Activity

Management principles and role responsibilities

For each of the principles identified by Everard and Morris (1996), try to identify how each category of curriculum manager will apply this in his or her role.

	Senior management	Middle management	Classroom teacher	Learning support	Student
Sets direction, aims and objectives					
Plans how progress will be made					
Organises resources to achieve goals economically					
Controls the process of measuring achievement					
Sets organisational standards					

Senior management

Senior managers in schools and colleges are commonly designated in the UK as the senior management team (SMT), although the term *leadership team* is starting to be used more widely. Membership of the SMT may vary according to the size and nature of the institution but, as a minimum, usually includes head/principal plus deputy head(s)/vice principal(s) and other senior staff as deemed appropriate. Thus the membership may be as small as three or as large as ten. In one- or two-teacher schools, all management responsibilities will, naturally, be carried by whoever is available. The success of these senior staff will depend partly upon their effectiveness as a team; we are here concerned specifically with their roles in managing the curriculum for learning and teaching. The key requirement for senior managers is to have a 'whole curriculum' view. While the professional autonomy of teachers remains a critical issue in operational management, overall strategies are not part and parcel of most teachers' working lives (Owen, 1992). Although effective leaders will involve staff in decisions about the curriculum, those staff's key tasks lie in teaching and managing effective learning at classroom level.

This whole curriculum view is one that sees what the institution provides,

> . . . in two distinct dimensions. It is a lateral view in the sense that it looks across the curriculum, to identify the totality of the learning that the curriculum offers a particular student at a particular stage. But it is also a longitudinal view in the sense that it adds continuity and progression in the student's learning experience, and searches out the gaps and repetition that the subject-centred approach inevitably produces (Duffy, 1988, pp. 116–17).

This two-dimensional view is vital for senior managers as it enables them to ensure that management processes such as record-keeping, monitoring and assessment are consistent and consistently applied, for the benefit of the individual student. In considering how curriculum management may be operated through the roles and responsibilities of the senior management team, two initial points may be made:

1. Whatever the individual roles, the effectiveness of the senior management team will be largely dependent upon the process of the team's working. Wallace and Hall's (1994) study of senior management teams illustrates the emphasis placed by schools on team dynamics and team development. Similarly, Bolam *et al.* (1993), in their report on effective management, stress the emphasis found on collaborative decision-making and shared leadership.

2. In the constantly changing world of the curriculum, the key feature of any structure for managing the curriculum might appear to be flexibility. All schools and colleges need to have core structures that can accommodate and meet changing demands.

Management of the curriculum, in any overt sense, may be seen through job descriptions and responsibilities allocation as being the province of some senior staff more than others but, collectively, the curriculum remains their key management responsibility.

Four main aspects, which need to be addressed if senior managers are to fulfil their roles, have been identified by Middlewood (2001) as:

- Having a view of the whole curriculum
- Ensuring accountability for high standards in learning and teaching
- Developing an appropriate culture and environment
- Being a role model for both learners and teachers.

◉ Reading

Now read 'Leadership of the curriculum: setting the vision', Chapter 7 in Middlewood, D. and Burton, N. (2001) *Managing the Curriculum*.

In this, David Middlewood considers the role of senior staff in leadership of the curriculum, which he considers to be the core purpose of the organisation.

❏ **Our comments**

Middlewood considers the role of senior staff is crucial and their actions will determine whether nationally imposed curricula are effective at the institutional level. Senior managers need to develop a view of the *whole* curriculum that ensures 'the whole is greater than the sum of the parts'. This strategic overview will not only include the analysis of data in order to provide a total picture of progress and achievement but will also allow gaps in provision to be identified and filled. In addition to developing an overview, senior managers are also required to ensure accountability and high standards, develop an appropriate culture and act as role model.

Whilst reading this chapter, you may have started to think how the senior management team in your own school or college addresses these key areas. If you are, yourself, part of the senior management team, it may be useful to reflect on how closely your own role and responsibilities match Middlewood's analysis. The power of individual senior managers to make a difference may rely on the willingness and ability of the headteacher or principal to delegate effectively.

Some of the issues senior staff need to manage will include the following:

- Providing a structure in which the whole student is considered, at individual, group and institutional levels.
- Making 'whole school/whole college' approaches, through policies, feasible.
- Responding to curriculum changes in an appropriate way.
- Ensuring internal and external accountability for curriculum delivery.
- Ensuring curriculum development is coherent, not piecemeal.

Curriculum mapping allows an overview to be developed that ensures the issues identified above are considered in a coherent manner. In operational terms, whichever structure is planned and managed, senior managers will need to address issues such as:

- Composition of teams
- Quality of team interactions
- Professional development of staff
- Ownership of developments in the curriculum
- Monitoring and evaluation of learning and teaching.

Middle management

Middle managers, as the name implies, are intermediate between senior staff and class teachers. They have to explain and interpret the policies of the SMT for colleagues in their teams and to present the views of these colleagues to senior staff – a 'bridging and brokering' role (Bennett, 1995). There may be some tension in this role as middle managers are sandwiched between the contrasting expectations of senior and more junior colleagues.

A current debate about middle managers concerns their contribution to the strategic planning for the whole institution. Research by Earley (1998, p. 148) indicates that middle managers in schools are primarily concerned with curriculum, and that the formation of strategy is 'unlikely to be seen as central' to their role, although the contribution of middle managers to shared decision-making is becoming increasingly important. In their research in FE colleges, Ainley and Bailey (1998, p. 61) comment that most middle managers felt that their role was 'to interpret SMT strategy in the best interests of teachers in their curriculum areas or Schools', although Lumby (2001b) indicates elements of dispersed leadership in the colleges she surveyed. Perhaps you would like to consider in your institution how strategy is formed: is it imposed from outside? If not, is it entirely the province of senior managers or do middle managers have a role?

Consideration of the role of middle managers requires an understanding of the concept of 'role'. It can be regarded as the behavioural aspect of the position, indicating how the role-holder acts in practice rather than what may be set down in formal documents such as the job description. The way(s) in which the role is performed depends on the role-holder's own preference, as well as the wider expectations of the 'role set'. The role set includes both the role-holder and those who interact with him or her, and the role is influenced by the assumptions of all those in the role set. For the head of department, the role set includes the headteacher, other members of the SMT, particularly the deputy or vice principal with responsibility for whole curriculum co-ordination, and teachers in the department. Where there are differences in the expectations of members of the role set, the incumbent is likely to experience role strain or role conflict. Some examples of role sets are provided by Wise (1999) and include:

- Staff within departments
- Head and SMT
- Students
- Advisers and inspectors
- Subject associations
- Other teaching staff
- Parents and guardians
- Governors.

Middle managers in schools and colleges are identified in relation to a variety of titles and roles. These are likely to include:

- Subject leader
- Course team leader
- Head of department
- Additional support co-ordinator
- Key skills co-ordinator
- Basic skills co-ordinator
- ICT co-ordinator
- Special needs co-ordinator.

All curriculum leaders, whatever their title or role, will need to possess skills and knowledge across a number of areas. Sergiovanni (1984) identifies three key areas:

1. Sound planning, time management and organisational skills.

2. Effective interpersonal and motivational skills, and a willingness to encourage participatory decision-making.

3. Professional expertise in terms of curriculum knowledge, support for the teaching team and the ability to lead staff development.

It may be useful to bear these in mind when looking at the roles and responsibilities in your own institution. Implied within Sergiovanni's key areas is successful classroom practice, since middle managers will also be expected to act as role models as well as managers of learning and teaching within their sphere of responsibility.

👁 *Reading*

Please now read Chapter 8 in Middlewood, D. and Burton, N. (2001) *Managing the Curriculum* **on the subject leader.**

In this chapter, Christine Wise and Hugh Busher review the subject leader's role and discuss a number of influences that affect how that role is conceived and performed.

❏ Our comments

The role of subject leader is described as 'multifaceted', working across boundaries and operating within a complex web of responsibilities and accountability. Subject leaders hold a key middle management position in the organisation and leadership has become an increasingly important part of their role.

Wise and Busher make the point that many of the models of the subject leader role focus on the structural aspects – tasks and responsibilities – and tend to neglect the relationships intrinsic to the role. A lack of clarity in defining the diverse role of subject leader leads to role ambiguity, stress and difficulty in fulfilling the demands of the job.

A shared culture that links subject, or department, cultures to the whole-school culture provides a supportive framework for improvements in learning and teaching, as does a shared understanding of, and commitment to, the prevalent ideology of the school or college. Subject development plans will benefit from a coherent view of department and whole-school aims and contribute to a more informed system of resource allocation.

This chapter discusses how progression can be facilitated within a prescribed system such as the English and Welsh National Curriculum to enable students to meet the benchmark levels of performance set by the DfES. Where schools have difficulties in ensuring adequate coverage, the subject leader needs to implement careful monitoring of curriculum delivery and utilise a variety of means to gather and use data to inform this monitoring. Subject leaders also have an important part to play in improving the quality of learning in their own subject areas by helping colleagues to improve the quality of their teaching. This implies that subject leaders, therefore, need to be good role models – the leading professional in their area.

In the UK, the role of subject leaders has been closely defined within a set of national standards (TTA, 1998). Bell and Ritchie (1999, p. 19) have taken these as the starting point to develop a more flexible framework that better reflects the complexity and scope of the subject leader's role:

> There are . . . dangers in trying to fix a model that lists every possible role in which a subject leader might become engaged, not least the fact that the model becomes too complicated and is not helpful. Rather we need a framework in which it is possible to identify roles as they develop and allows scope for the model to evolve as time and place change. In [the table] we have attempted to set out the variety and range of roles subject leaders may undertake but do not regard the list as being fixed. On the contrary we would suggest that the number of combinations is almost endless.

Bell and Ritchie's table is reproduced here as Table 3.1. The list of responsibilities is a daunting one, but the associated roles and tasks may help you to see more clearly how this may be related to your own institution and/or personal role. Although the key areas defined in the table are specifically related to subject leader responsibilities in schools, many of the associated tasks will also be familiar to middle managers in colleges of further education. FENTO (2000), the national body charged with defining management standards in further education in the UK, has produced a breakdown of middle manager responsibilities, the main headings for which are almost identical to those of Bell and Ritchie:

- Develop strategic practice

- Develop and sustain learning and the learning environment

- Lead teams and the individual

- Manage resources.

Lumby (2001b), in looking at the relationship of the management level to the leadership focus within colleges, finds that the middle management focus is on the implementation of the curriculum, which will involve many of the roles and tasks detailed by Bell and Ritchie. However, Briggs (2001b, p. 234), in a survey of middle managers from 13 FE colleges in England, found that:

> These managers were well aware of the demands of the 'new managerialism' (Randle and Brady, 1996), showing market awareness, spending time setting targets and measuring against performance indicators. Yet there was also a real concern for providing academic leadership within their department; a sign that they were attempting to straddle the professional/managerial divide. In a variety of contexts, all spoke about the stresses of their role, and the ways in which their lives had been affected.

The main issues that concerned these middle managers in further education are also of concern to middle managers in schools, namely: concerns about the size and complexity of their role and the extent of their responsibilities. A further anxiety surrounded the lack of role definition, which they felt undermined their autonomy and authority.

Reading

Before going on to look at classroom-based management, you should now read Les Bell's chapter on cross-curriculum co-ordination, Chapter 9 of Middlewood, D. and Burton, N. (2001) *Managing the Curriculum*, paying particular attention to what he has to say about the need for new management structures.

❏ Our comments

Bell makes the point that there is a fundamental incompatibility between the generally accepted aims of formal education: socialising children, academic achievement, developing individual potential. Cross-curriculum co-ordinators have the responsibility of weaving these aims into a coherent whole, but the tensions inherent in a subject-based curriculum pose considerable challenges. Some work has been done on introducing core skills across subject boundaries (literacy would be a good example of this) but 'thematic' curricula have not yet been established.

The cross-curricular role will need to shift from the 'reactive aspects of resource management towards the proactive consultant and critical friend functions'. There are, of course, resource implications in developing this role: time to work with colleagues is a major factor and not always available, especially in small schools. Bell also highlights the need for stronger role definition and status for co-ordinators, if policy implementation is to be successful.

Table 3.1 Responsibilities, roles and tasks of subject leaders

Key areas are	Responsibilities to	Roles involved	Tasks include
Strategic direction and development of the subject – to develop and implement subject policies, plans, targets and practices	• Develop and implement policies and practices • Create and maintain a climate of positive attitudes and confidence in teaching • Establish shared understanding of the importance and role of the subject • Identify and plan for supporting underachieving pupils • Analyse and interpret appropriate data, research and inspection evidence • Establish short-, medium- and long-term plans for development and resourcing of the subject • Monitor progress in achieving plans and targets and evaluate effects to inform further improvement	Leader Policy-maker Initiator Planner Advocate Negotiator Analyst Decision-maker Delegator Evaluator	• Auditing the subject • Analysing and evaluating data and evidence • Talking with the headteacher, colleagues and governors • Seeking appropriate advice • Agreeing aims, targets, criteria for success and deadlines • Preparing action plans • Documenting policies and plans
Teaching and learning – to secure and sustain effective teaching of the subject, evaluate the quality of teaching and standards of pupils' achievements and set targets for improvement	• Ensure curriculum coverage, continuity and progression for all pupils • Ensure teachers understand and communicate objectives and sequence of teaching and learning • Provide guidance on teaching and learning methods to meet pupil and subject needs • Ensure development of literacy, numeracy and ICT skills through the subject • Establish and implement policies and practices for assessing, recording and reporting • Ensure information on pupils' achievement is used to secure progress • Set expectations for staff and pupils and evaluate progress and achievement of all pupils • Evaluate teaching, identify good practice and act to improve the quality of teaching • Ensure development of pupils' individual and collaborative study skills • Ensure teachers are aware of subject's contribution to the pupils' understanding of citizenship	Adviser Planner Educator Consultant Co-ordinator Learner Subject 'expert'	• Preparing and documenting schemes of work, assessments, records and reports • Talking with and advising colleagues on activities and lessons • Suggesting ideas and starting points • Supporting knowledge and understanding • Talking to outside contacts • Putting up displays and promoting the subject • Check links with other areas of the curriculum

Key areas are	Responsibilities to	Roles involved	Tasks include
	• Ensure teachers can recognise and deal with racial stereotyping • Establish partnership and involvement of parents • Develop links with the community, business and industry		
Leading and managing staff – to provide to all those with involvement in the teaching or support of the subject, the support, challenge information and development necessary to sustain motivation and secure improvement in teaching	• Help staff achieve constructive working relationships with pupils • Establish expectations and constructive working relationships among staff • Sustain motivation of themselves and colleagues • Appraise staff, if appropriate • Audit training needs • Lead professional development and co-ordinate provision • Ensure trainees and NQTs are supported to achieve appropriate standards • Enable colleagues to achieve expertise in subject teaching • Work with SENCO to develop IEPs • Ensure headteacher, senior managers and governors are well informed	Leader Manager Motivator Negotiator Collaborator Delegator Diplomat Mediator Listener Confidant Critical friend Educator Learner	• Planning, arranging and running INSET • Working alongside colleagues in classrooms • Listening to colleagues • Keeping colleagues up to date • Presenting subject to governors
Efficient and effective deployment of staff and resources – to identify appropriate resources for the subject and ensure they are used efficiently, effectively and safely	• Establish and advise on all resource needs and allocate subject resources efficiently • Advise on the best use of colleagues • Ensure effective and efficient management and organisation of learning resources, including ICT • Maintain existing resources and explore opportunities to develop and incorporate new ones • Use accommodation to create a stimulating environment • Ensure a safe working and learning environment	Manager Organiser Planner Provider Facilitator Technician	• Selecting and ordering materials and equipment • Organising storage and making sure resources are accessible • Demonstrating use of equipment • Finding out about new resources • Monitoring the budget • Auditing resources • Finding alternative ways of using the environment • Assessing risks with equipment and activities

Source: Bell and Ritchie (1999, pp. 16–18)

Classroom-based management

There are at least two key players in the management of learning and teaching at classroom level: student and teacher. This traditional configuration may be supplemented by the addition of one or more curriculum or learning support staff. The controlling member of this learning trio will be the class teacher, who retains the responsibility for ensuring successful learning takes place. In Chapter 12 of Middlewood and Burton (2001), David Middlewood examines the rationale for employing curriculum support staff and provides the following arguments in favour of their use:

1. Gives the teacher more time to concentrate on using his or her expertise.

2. Assists in the effective preparation and deployment of resources.

3. Enables more effective and efficient organisation of learners.

He points out that, whilst there are marked differences in the nature and range of work carried out by support staff across phases of education, there are some common features that apply to all. These include working alongside students who have special needs, giving extra help to individuals or small groups withdrawn from lessons, supporting teachers in the delivery of lessons and providing verbal reports of student progress.

As the principal manager in the classroom, the teacher will be responsible for all aspects of planning, delivery and evaluation of the learning process. To ensure this happens, he or she will delegate some responsibilities to the student and to any classroom assistants available. In primary schools, this tripartite relationship will tend to be contained predominantly within one classroom but, in secondary schools and colleges of further education, the relationship will be part of a wider network of classes and teachers that goes to make up the total learning experience of individual students. In this situation, support staff may be able to take on a bridging role if they are employed to support individuals or groups of students with, say, special needs.

❏ Our comments

The teacher's responsibility, as the acknowledged leader in classroom-based management, will be evident across all areas. The involvement of support staff and students will depend, to a large extent, on the culture of the classroom and the participative ethos of the school.

Support staff in some situations will have a greater role to play than in others. In special schools, for example, learning support assistants will often be professionals in their own right (such as qualified nursery nurses) and will, therefore, be expected to take on greater responsibilities than untrained staff working in other contexts.

Students in primary schools will have less responsibility for managing their own learning than students in further education, but even with younger children there is still scope for involving them at some level, perhaps by encouraging them to engage in self-assessment or certainly by making clear their role in maintaining good discipline in the classroom.

Stoll and Fink (1996), commenting on the idea of 'pupils as partners', make the point that school is as much the workplace for students as it is for teachers. They cite Levin (1994, p. 759), who states that students are 'much more than raw materials, since their ideas and behaviour have an enormous influence on how the process of education unfolds'. They go on to say:

> Our own work suggests that many teachers are resistant to the notion of partnership which includes pupils. Our questionnaires to teachers and students at both the primary and secondary levels not only revealed little student involvement in school decision making but also reflected teachers' belief that students should not be involved (Stoll and Fink, 1996, p. 139).

Activity

Working together to support learning and teaching

This activity asks you to identify the relative responsibilities of teacher, student and support staff in promoting learning and participation in the classroom. Tick the appropriate box for each statement to indicate who has a responsibility in this area, adding comments as you wish.

Area	Teacher	Student	Support	Comments
Making role expectations clear				
Deciding teaching approaches				
Producing resources				
Giving feedback on performance				
Maintaining discipline				
Record-keeping				
Assessment				
Planning				
Liaison with other staff				
Identifying development needs				

Whilst quality assurance procedures in UK further education require colleges to take student views into account, Lumby (2001a, p. 123) notes that, in practice, students are not generally in a position to make decisions about their learning: 'Learners may influence the nature and course of their learning more than previously, but there is still a need for a partnership where the interests of the student are partly represented by the individual and partly by the staff who support their learning'. This links with the views of Middlewood (2001), who introduces the idea of the teacher as 'co-learner, exploring opportunities with the student' and thus providing a powerful role model for life-long learning.

Some of the issues raised in this section are also discussed in Chapter 2, particularly in the sections on 'Teaching strategies' and 'Classroom climate'. You may like to consider the role of the student in the light of the factors considered in these earlier sections of the book.

In the next section we move from the wider, organisational level of curriculum management to a deeper consideration of the processes involved in learning and teaching, through an examination of planning, assessment and evaluation procedures.

❑ **Key learning points**

- Management of the curriculum is concerned with the *what* and the *how* of learning and teaching.

- Attention needs to be given to assessment and evaluation of the processes in place, in order to ensure what is happening is effective.

- An agreed framework for curriculum management enables decisions to be made about content, delivery, resources, responsibilities, etc.

- A new paradigm of curriculum management emphasises a collegial approach, which shares responsibility across a wider base.

- Models of curriculum management will reflect the culture and values of the institution as well as the constraints that operate at all levels.

- Roles and responsibilities for curriculum management may operate through a hierarchical or collaborative model and involve few or many members of the organisation. Students are beginning to be included in managing their own learning at an earlier stage of their schooling.

Managing the learning process

In the first chapter we considered what it is that makes up a curriculum, and we looked at the local and national influences that are brought to bear on its content and delivery. Once the broad parameters of the curriculum have been defined – by government, by academic, religious or cultural leaders, by representatives from business and industry, by the schools and colleges themselves – the learning process for the students and children has to be planned, monitored and evaluated, and their learning assessed. These processes are necessary, not just because they aid the logistics of teaching but because of the levels of accountability within which schools and colleges operate.

They are accountable to those who provide their funding: parents, students, the government and, through the government, the population as a whole. They are accountable to their 'market': all those who benefit from the education provided. They have a particular accountability to their profession, a responsibility to their peers and their students to uphold high professional standards, and they are more broadly accountable for their contribution to the culture of the country and the community (based on Scott, 1989). This means that, although individual teachers, guided by their professional status, may choose one syllabus or set of lesson material over another, or that a college, guided by the cultural and market needs of its community, will choose to specialise in a particular aspect of education or training, what teachers and students do is carried out within sight and hearing of the public, and the processes within the school or college must stand up to public scrutiny. Therefore, processes of monitoring and evaluation are carried out, both internally by school or college staff, and externally by inspectors or verifiers.

The sections that follow consider a set of related activities essential to the management of the learning and teaching process. These are as follows:

- *Planning* – of curricula, learning programmes or special projects to support learning.
- *Assessment* – of student learning.
- *Evaluation* – of the effectiveness of learning programmes and teaching activities against agreed criteria.
- *Monitoring* – the collection of data on the agreed criteria to be used in evaluation.

These activities of planning, assessment, monitoring and evaluation are often represented as a cyclical model. One such cycle for curriculum provision is represented here in Figure 3.5.

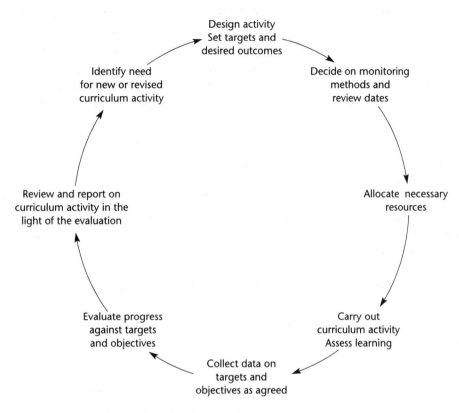

Figure 3.5 Planning, monitoring and evaluating curriculum activities

As we consider the cycle, a feature that soon emerges is the interdependency of the constituent activities. *Planning*, which largely occupies the cells labelled 'identify need', 'design activity', 'decide on monitoring' and 'allocate resources', is seen to depend upon the evaluation of previous activity and includes consideration of the monitoring and subsequent review processes. *Assessment* – of individual students – occupies only part of one cell but contributes vitally to the evaluation of student achievement as a whole and the success of the curriculum venture. *Evaluation* and its supporting activity, *monitoring*, permeate the whole cycle. It is the evaluation of the learning process that gives credibility to the planning cycle and, yet, as we shall see, it is often neglected.

The planning of learning and teaching

Looking back upon primary school curriculum provision in the UK in the years before the introduction of a national curriculum, the writers of a government-initiated report commented:

> Much school planning . . . amounted to little more than an attempt to list the content to be covered . . . With the introduction of the National Curriculum and the School Development Plan initiative, there has been a recognition that teachers must plan together to ensure consistency and progression . . . All teachers need time to plan and prepare their work (Alexander *et al.*, 1992, p. 20).

It seems at first ironic that under a system where schools largely devised their own curriculum there was less coherent planning than under the later system where a curriculum was imposed by central government. What made the difference was an increased awareness of accountability, together with a new government imperative upon schools and colleges to plan.

Where planning has been introduced, and the planning process evaluated, interesting findings can emerge. An evaluation of factors affecting the effectiveness of planning in Hong Kong schools (Wong *et al.*, 1998) revealed that *built-in flexibility* and *flexibility through evaluation* are good predictors of positive outcomes for planning. The researchers comment that 'when a plan is designed with alternatives for some foreseeable circumstances, or is written in sufficiently general terms to allow for some discretion in implementation for different situations, it is reasonable to find that both of these practices make sense to teachers' (Wong *et al.*, p. 76). Similarly: 'If a plan is designed with options to cater for different environments, it is likely that the preparation process has involved some scanning of possible future environmental conditions' (Wong *et al.*, p. 77). *Flexibility through professional autonomy* did not correlate well with positive outcomes of planning: the researchers hypothesise that either Hong Kong teachers are not accustomed to professional freedom or that 'changes initiated by individual teachers in these circumstances may be largely uncoordinated' (Wong *et al.*). Both these emergent findings are brought together in the recommendation that teachers should be encouraged and helped to participate in planning. Their knowledge and experience, both of their subject and of the external environment, will result in more realistic goals being set. Moreover, if the built-in flexibility has to be applied to the situation, 'teachers who have been involved in the planning process are well prepared for changes . . .' (Wong *et al.*, p. 78).

This experience – of the applicability of teacher knowledge and of the need for flexibility to accommodate expected (seen) and unseen future circumstances – should be borne in mind when considering planning activities, otherwise there is a danger the processes become mechanistic and ultimately meaningless.

◉ *Reading*

For a helpful review of the topic of curriculum planning, please read the chapter by Neil Burton, 'Managing the planning of learning and teaching', Chapter 4 in Middlewood, D. and Burton, N. (2001) *Managing the Curriculum*. As you read, pay particular attention to the grid (4.1) he discusses and start to work out its relevance to your own planning activities.

As has been implied in the account of the Hong Kong research cited above, the planning activities described here take place within the framework of the strategic planning of the school or college and are a constituent activity of it. You may therefore wish also to consult Chapter 4: ('Leadership and strategy') by Cheng Yin Cheong in Bush, T. and Bell, L. (2002) *The Principles and Practice of Educational Management*.

❏ **Our comments**

Burton's grid highlights the importance at every level of the planning process of resource issues, management issues and expectation or progression issues. The sequence of ideas in the chapter is highlighted in the discussion below.

❑ Resource issues

At an *institutional* level, this will largely concern the level of incoming resource and the institution-wide structures that carry that resource to where it is needed (i.e. the individual learner). Planning might involve the identification of additional, perhaps specialised, sources of funding, or improved use by the institution of the staff, buildings and funds it has. For further discussion in this area, read the chapter 'The management of resources for learning', Chapter 13 of Middlewood and Burton (2001).

At the *curriculum area* level, the focus will be on the appropriate deployment of teachers and assistants, teacher time and departmental funds. In many cases, this will involve liaison with other curriculum areas (for example, to negotiate appropriate allocation of shared staff or specialist accommodation across the institution). Planning at the *class group* and *individual student* levels should inform planning at curriculum area level. For example, provision for students in small classes, such as those following minority subjects in the curriculum or those with individual learning needs, has to be assessed and built into the curriculum area plan. It can be seen from this brief outline that, starting with the individual student, elements of each 'layer' of planning become aggregated within the layer 'above'.

A worked example might be that the college or school wishes to raise student achievement in a particular subject. The underachieving students have to be identified and their needs assessed in terms of resources. These resources have to be improved. This may have implications for staff development if the problem lies with the quality of teaching, or additional resources may need to be found. These may be diverted from other parts of the identified curriculum area, diverted from other curriculum areas – for example, in terms of extra time on the timetable or access to 'shared' staffing – or found from new sources external to the institution.

❑ Management issues

The function of planning at the *institutional* level would be through effective strategic planning and target-setting, and through management structures that enable departmental or phase-specific development planning to take place in congruence with the strategic plan. This development planning would take place at the *curriculum area* level by groupings of staff representing age-related phases of education in primary schools, curriculum areas or subjects in secondary schools, or course or programme area in post-compulsory education.

In school environments, particularly primary schools, the identity of the individual class is strong and provides a focus for decision-making, target-setting and essential communications. In secondary schools, where students may belong to more than one 'class group' in a given day, planning is nevertheless often focused upon the achievement of individual groups. In post-compulsory education, whilst the class group would form an important social identity for the individual student, the management of planning would largely take place at the level of the course or programme of learning. In all phases, maintaining an efficient flow of information about *individual students* is an essential part of the management of planning, most particularly for students with special needs who often have an individual education plan that addresses their specific requirements.

❑ Expectation and progression issues

Planning for progression is easiest to conceptualise from the perspective of the *individual student*. Each student, however young or old, has expectations of learning and potential progression routes from his or her current phase of learning. For the youngest, the expectations may largely be framed by the teacher or parent, whilst the older, more autonomous learner will have his or her own expectations and plans for the future. These 'future hopes' form an essential part of the planning process: aggregated at *class*, *curriculum* and *institutional* levels of planning, they are the essential ingredient of the planning question: 'Where would we like to be in the future?'

Activity

Smart planning

All the planning activities above involve some form of target-setting. A commonly used concept is that of SMART targets:

Strategic

Measurable

Achievable

Realistic and

Time-constrained.

This has been developed further for educational settings by Davies and Ellison (1999, p. 123) as **SMARTIES**, using the original five elements quoted above plus:

Interesting

Exciting

Success-orientated.

Draft a set of SMART (or SMARTIES) targets for a school or college-wide initiative, for planning a specific classroom-based innovation or for monitoring learner progress. If you work in a special school, devise a set of group targets that take account of individual student targets.

❏ Our comments

Unless you are used to setting targets in this way, you probably found the activity quite difficult. What was the strategic aim of what you planned, and how will you measure your achievement or that of your learners? Working within time constraints helps us to be realistic in what we plan, and consideration of the available resource – of time, money and effort – helps to set the development within achievable limits.

Within a special school context, the synthesis of individual and group targets is dependent on how well the programme of work can be differentiated to take account of different needs within the group.

When faced with a planning task, find out what the institution's SMART targets are for this kind of development: if they – or something like them – do not exist, your own planning process may lack coherence.

Assessment of student and pupil learning

The next element in the cycle – assessment of learning – is a concept that can either be dealt with simply:

- Can the learners demonstrate they have learned what the curriculum directed they should learn?

or impossibly:

- What have these children or students learned?

The second question opens up vast areas of learning that will never be assessed or that may be assessed at a later date in a different context; it also addresses the breadth of the curricula discussed in Chapter 1: rhetorical, planned, delivered and received. However, whilst acknowledging this is by far the more interesting question of the two, we shall return, for the sake of manageability, to the first one.

Assessment can be *internal* or *external* to the institution; it can be *formative* (to inform on progress and aid improvement) or *summative* (to record the level reached at the end of a block of learning or a whole course). It can operate through taking a *sample* of the student's learning or it can attempt to assess the *whole*. It can be *continuous* (happening all the time), *modular* (happening at the end of discrete blocks of learning) or *terminal* (at the end of the course). It can be carried out through a range of strategies, such as tutor observation of activities; completion of reflective journals, assignments or written tests; creation of artefacts or works of art, including music; or oral presentation, performance or participation in discussion. It can be imposed as an external judgement or carried out jointly with the learner.

If a school or college has the freedom to devise its own assessment schemes, these are some of the choices of assessment mode that will be involved. Even if summative assessment – for the purposes of accreditation – is designed and 'imposed' from outside, formative assessment, to guide the learning process, happens through many of the above activities in each classroom every day, and a school or college may also devise its own periodic formative and summative assessments based upon a range of these strategies.

Stoll and Fink (1996, p. 124) suggest there may be a tendency for teachers to assess mainly through the ways in which they themselves were assessed. They assert that all practitioners need to become more 'assessment literate' and that effective assessment is based upon answers to the following questions:

- Are these the best assessment practices to assess this learning outcome?
- How well does this assessment sample students' achievement?
- Do the students understand the achievement targets and the assessment methods?
- Does this assessment assess outcomes that matter?
- Are assessment strategies fair for all students?
- How are the resulting data to be presented?
- Who will have access to the data?
- How will they be reported and to whom?

These last two questions begin to lead on to what will be discussed later in this section: the evaluation of the learning process.

Rather than base the assessment around 'teacher intention' or the content of the curriculum, Stoll and Fink (1996, pp. 124–25) advocate a focus on the learning outcomes students and pupils are expected to achieve. During the assessment process, learners can be *compared to each other, compared with predetermined criteria* for their age or stage of learning, or learners' *individual progress* can be gauged by assessing their skills or knowledge at both the beginning and end of the programme of learning. This last approach is the most equitable and learner focused; however, it is also the most costly of time and assessor skills.

Planning a framework of assessment – whether on a whole-school, school department or college programme basis – is important, not only in providing a coherent, continued assessment process for the learner but also to support evaluation of the learning and teaching process. The assessment framework for a school comprising nursery and primary years 1–6 is cited by MacGilchrist *et al.* (1997, p. 76):

a. Regular testing and assessment from nursery to year 6

b. Teachers have an assessment focus on their weekly plans

c. Cumulative records and work samples are kept from 3–11 years

d. There is an individual 'Progress Chart' for each child which records certain tests and assessments

e. An abstract reasoning test is given in year 3 to identify underachievement

f. Notes on special needs, including Individual Educational Plans, are kept.

The focus here is on the individual child: aggregated records could also be used to assess trends and patterns in learning at the school.

Within the limits of their understanding it is important that learning goals, assessment methods and criteria are shared with the learners and, where appropriate, their parents. The assessment process is carried out for the benefit of the learners to acknowledge their achievements and to indicate areas of understanding still to be developed. It is therefore important they are involved as fully as possible and understand the process. In the case of young children, assessment may be 'disguised' as play or as routine classroom activity: even so, their achievements can be celebrated and areas of concern discussed with them or with their parents. Older learners may benefit from a self-assessment element being included to heighten personal awareness of their progress. This could be in the form of a reflective diary or preparation for developmental discussion with the tutor.

Issues of *equity* arise from some of the questions posed above: 'Are assessment strategies fair for all pupils?' 'How will the resulting data be presented?' The answer to the first question will almost certainly be 'no' unless assessment is individually designed for each learner; therefore it is important to take note of the second question. If some learners' achievements have already been underestimated, for example because they are nervous about exams or have limited language skills, this error can be compounded when results are 'published' within and outside the school or used as a measure of the student's worth – or even the worth of the institution.

The issue of assessing 'outcomes that matter' is also an important and difficult one. A national or regionally directed curriculum will be directed towards the outcomes deemed important by the state or the region, and these are the outcomes that will be tested. Stoll and Fink (1996, p. 125) ask: 'Should standards be based on expert opinion, or what pupils actually do, or based on real-world demands?' The assessment of vocational qualifications in the UK might be seen as attempting to do all three: performance criteria are set by 'lead bodies' of experts, based upon the requirements of business and industry, and learners are assessed by what they 'can do', often in real or simulated working conditions.

Activity

Assessing progress

How do you assess your learners' progress? List the different strategies you know to be in operation at your school or college and consider their appropriateness for assessing learning outcomes.

❑ Our comments

Your internal assessment strategies may mirror those that are externally imposed: in this way you prepare the children and students for the 'real thing'. However, thinking about particular learning outcomes – a child's development of motor skills; a pupil's understanding of a scientific concept; a learner's confidence in using a foreign language; a student's ability to think through a problem – may lead you to devise specific ways of testing these skills to enable you to be confident they have been achieved.

Monitoring curriculum activities

A major purpose of the assessment activities considered above is to monitor student progress, at individual, group, institutional or even national level. The information gained through student assessment thus feeds into the next process we discuss, the monitoring of curriculum activities: the planned and purposeful collection of information in order to evaluate progress towards targets. Monitoring might be carried out to evaluate a specific curriculum activity, perhaps the teaching of a new subject or the progress of a group of learners who have been giving concern, or it might involve collecting information across a department or the whole institution to ensure appropriate standards are being maintained. When used to evaluate how well institutions are performing, it can help to answer the question: 'Do we do what we say we do?' When used to evaluate new developments, it can provide valuable information in response to the question: 'Are we getting there?' (Hardie, 2001, p. 87). As part of the evaluation process, monitoring contributes towards 'making judgments about the worth of an activity by systematically and openly collecting and analysing information about it, and relating to explicit objectives, criteria and values' (Aspinwall *et al.*, 1992, p. 2).

In Figure 3.5 ('Planning, monitoring and evaluating curriculum activities'), with which we began this section, *Decide on monitoring methods and review dates* is included in the planning activities, and *Collect data on targets and objectives as agreed* appears later in the cycle as the curriculum activity proceeds. In order to evaluate a curriculum activity, therefore, targets and objectives have to be set in advance, performance criteria agreed to ensure clarity of aspirations and achievement, and data systematically collected.

👁 *Reading*

Please read the chapter by Brian Hardie 'Managing monitoring of the curriculum', Chapter 5 in Middlewood, D. and Burton, N. (2001) *Managing the Curriculum*.

Note his definition of monitoring, and watch out for the amazing MACFEWOI! acronym that guides you through the target-setting process. As you read, consider what internal monitoring processes are carried out at your school or college. What is your role in monitoring curriculum provision?

❑ Our comments

Hardie points out that *informal monitoring* is a natural part of the teaching process. Such factors as student attendance, attention, interaction and application to tasks will all be noted by an effective teacher, whether or not they are being formally monitored. Likewise informal monitoring of colleagues might include observation of students as they leave the teaching room, noting the quality of student work displayed or paying attention to the nature of teachers' comments about their students. In both these cases, the informal monitoring might lead to supportive or remedial action. However, it is the open, planned and systematic activity of monitoring that produces valid data for evaluation purposes.

Hardie describes monitoring as a questioning activity – often asking the questions people don't want to be asked. Like any process of research, it is undertaken to find out what is really happening and, like research, it requires data. Stoll and Fink (1996, p. 172) stress the importance of *baseline data*: 'Baseline data are vital and are an often neglected part of improvement initiatives.' They answer the planning question: 'Where are we now?' MacGilchrist *et al.* (1997) talk of the need to collect baseline information about children when they enter school – how else can their progress over time be measured?

Other essential data are those that supply information against *performance indicators*: 'An indicator is a single or composite statistic which reflects the health of an educational system, and can be reliably and repeatedly obtained' (Stoll and Fink, 1996, p. 183). They are carefully chosen, measurable proxies for the thing to be monitored: for example, accuracy in spelling a list of commonly used words could be one of a number of performance indicators for literacy; level of student satisfaction on a student perception questionnaire could be one of a set of performance indicators for teaching quality. It is worth remembering that, if too few performance indicators are set, the validity of the judgement is undermined: if too many, the process becomes impossible.

A further activity that aids monitoring is *benchmarking*. One example of this is where the data collected at the school or college are submitted to an outside agency, which both collects the data from the institution and possesses contextual information about it (for example, size, curriculum offered, social conditions in the area). In the case of examination results, a school's achievements can be benchmarked against the whole group of schools submitting data or against schools operating under like conditions. In the case of resources spent, a college's expenditure on different budget areas – teaching, support staffing, library, building maintenance – can be compared with others of similar size and curriculum provision. Whether the benchmarking is carried out by national or local government agencies or by private contractors, analysis of the aggregated monitoring data from the whole group can be fed back to the individual institution to enable it to answer the question 'Where are we now?' in relation to other schools and colleges.

Not every activity can be monitored, or the business of learning and teaching would never be done; it is important therefore to choose a focus and to choose one that will be valuable to the institution or to a group within it. Where data are already available and are valid for the chosen purpose, they should be used to prevent an overload of data-collection activity. Sometimes, however, it can be useful to collect fresh data that will shed new light on the activity being monitored. For example, when a formal process of self-assessment was instituted in UK further education colleges in the 1990s, in some colleges data were collected systematically for the first time on student satisfaction: with their course teaching, with learning resources, with provision for student support.

Hardie (2001) points out the importance of reporting and acting on monitoring – this is the process of evaluation, to which we turn next.

The evaluation of learning

The evaluation activities of a school or college will be, directly or indirectly, focused upon learning. A further education college might evaluate the effectiveness of its links with industry, a special school its multidisciplinary support systems, a secondary school the effectiveness of its timetabling framework, a primary school its links with parents: all these examples are of phenomena 'just outside' the main business of learning and teaching, yet are as essential to the process as activities more commonly evaluated: student progress in individual subject areas, teacher effectiveness in the classroom or children's response to a new curriculum approach. The purpose of evaluation, in the context of managing education, is to enhance the experience of learning.

👁 *Reading*

Please read the chapter by Margaret Preedy, 'Curriculum evaluation: measuring what we value', Chapter 6 in Middlewood, D. and Burton, N. (2001) *Managing the Curriculum*.

Note the distinctions she makes between different types of evaluation, and who is involved in the process. It is sometimes claimed evaluation is the 'missing link' in education: we may plan and carry through an activity and may even monitor its progress to completion but are reluctant to evaluate it. Is this true in your organisation?

❏ Our comments

Evaluation, like assessment, can be formative or summative, internal or external to the institution. It can therefore be used to judge a *process* – the teaching of an individual teacher or subject, the progress of a development project – whilst it is happening in order that necessary adjustments and improvements can be made. In this way it can be used developmentally to manage change. Or it can be used to judge a *product*: did this year's students succeed as well as we expected? Did the ICT staff training result in an increase in teacher confidence and use of ICT? Often, the questions are asked internally, at whole-institutional level; at departmental level; at single class level; sometimes they are asked by external representatives of the bodies to whom teachers and managers are accountable (for example, by government inspectors or representatives from industry). Unlike assessment, evaluation serves to make a *judgement*. If monitoring seeks to answer the question: 'Are we doing what we say we are doing?' evaluation asks: 'Are we doing it well enough?'

Who should be involved? For internal evaluation, a simple answer might be: everyone who is involved in the process being evaluated – and that includes the students. As Preedy observes (2001, p. 99), there are many reasons for including them:

- They are the intended beneficiaries of the programme
- Only they can tell us about the *received* curriculum
- They can provide helpful and constructive feedback
- There is a strong democratic and moral case for including them
- Seeking student views encourages student ownership of the norms and values of the institution: this is particularly important in the case of disaffected students
- Student skills in reflection and evaluation are developed during the process of consultation.

Equally, internal evaluation of the work of the department or of an individual teacher would include data collection and reflection and analysis by the department or individual concerned. Where internal evaluation is simply 'done to' an individual or a group, it is likely to be perceived as a threat and result in demotivation.

Preedy (2001, p. 96) poses a number of key questions that continue the principle of *selection* of areas for scrutiny and the setting of agreed *evidence sets*, *criteria* and *timescales* before the process starts, which were discussed in the section on monitoring. In addition to these principles, she adds consideration of *roles*: who will be involved? Who will make the judgements?

Thomas (1985) analyses this question through a useful set of criteria. Although his analysis was carried out some time ago, it is still useful in understanding relationships in evaluation. Evaluation is presented as two continua of relationships, as set out in Figures 3.6 and 3.7.

CRITERIA CONTINUUM

Negotiated criteria

Setting own or
negotiated criteria

Imposed criteria

Criteria may not match
desired objectives

JUDGEMENT CONTINUUM

Open judgement

Those being evaluated
have a part in preparing
final evaluative statement

Closed judgement

Those being evaluated
have no part in preparing
final evaluative statement

Figure 3.6 Evaluation relationships
Source: After Thomas (1985, p. 386)

In Figure 3.6 we see evaluation relationships in terms of the questions: 'Who sets the criteria?' and 'Who makes the judgements?' If the individual, the department or the institution being evaluated has some role in setting the criteria, the match between the criteria set and the objectives of the evaluation may be closer and the process more valued. Likewise, the more involved the subject of the evaluation is with the judgement, the more likely he or she is to 'own' and act on the results.

These two continua can then be used to form a matrix for identifying the model of conduct in operation during a particular evaluation process, as in Figure 3.7. Where closed judgement and imposed criteria predominate, an inspectorial relationship will prevail; closed judgement and negotiated criteria are a feature of a consultative model – criteria have been agreed with the consultant but the judgement process is closed; open judgement and negotiated criteria are the model for evaluation for professional development – of the individual or the institution; in the marketing model, criteria are imposed on the process, but the judgement to be made will be open.

These two figures from Thomas (1985) thus present us with a way of exploring Preedy's questions (2001, p. 96) about roles and criteria-setting in evaluation. As a final, most important, question, Preedy asks: 'What action will be taken as a result of the evaluation findings?' Monitoring and evalua-

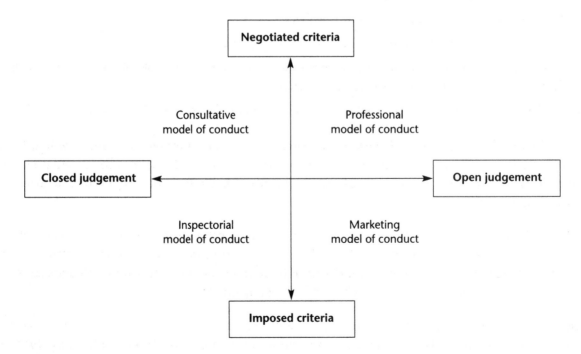

Figure 3.7 Matrix of evaluation relationships
Source: Thomas (1985, p. 386)

tion that does not result in action breaks the cycle of planning for improvement we have been considering in this section. In the case of evaluation of a successfully completed project, the action may involve celebration and dissemination of understanding of 'what made it work', together with the inevitable 'lessons to be learned'. The evaluation of an ongoing process – links with local employers, achievements in external examinations, developing particular pupil skills – if successfully shared within the school or college, becomes embedded in the collective learning experience and expertise of the staff as they approach the next cycle of this activity. The activities of dissemination and 'sharing' take time and collective engagement with the topic; in many cases the school or college working year only allows them a brief place.

A concept relevant here is that of *double-loop learning*. Clarke (2000, p. 139) represents this as in Figure 3.8. The learner – an individual, a department, an institution – plans, carries out and evaluates an activity in the way we have been discussing. It then reviews the purposes and values of the activity in the light of the evaluation that has taken place and feeds this learning back into the activity loop. The result is better informed, empowered action.

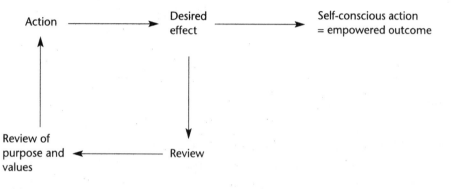

Figure 3.8 Double-loop learning
Source: Clarke (2000, p. 139)

Processes of *external evaluation*, such as *inspection*, include the external setting of criteria and targets, the collection of data and the monitoring of processes to be judged, and judgements being made upon the worth of the process evaluated. The extent to which the stakeholders (the teachers, learners and managers) are involved in the judgement, and know of the performance criteria, will vary according to circumstance.

Sometimes, as in UK post-compulsory institutions, one institution will be inspected and evaluated by a number of bodies, each making judgements against their own criteria. Where *self-assessment* is part of the process, the stakeholders can be involved and the school or college can benefit from the self-reflective process. Here the 'inspectorial' mode of conduct and the 'professional' mode of conduct referred to above are at least partially reconciled. As one UK further education senior manager comments in Ainley and Bailey (1997, p. 54), when considering the improvements an increased level of accountability has brought to colleges: 'I just think that the focus is sharper and I think people are more rigorous about what they give to young people and adults these days.'

In a comparative study of school inspection practice in seven countries, CERI (1995) identifies the status of teachers in the different countries as an important factor in the way inspection systems are set up: 'In Germany, France, and, to a certain extent, Sweden, a long training with a respected qualification, followed by relatively high pay and good conditions leads to a strong sense of professionalism in carrying out the functions of a teacher, which in those countries is well-established and understood' (CERI, 1995, p. 43). Therefore, the governments put less pressure upon teachers – indeed in Germany, at the date of the report, schools were not inspected at all.

In England, the USA and, to a lesser extent, New Zealand, teachers have relatively low pay and status, government-instigated educational reforms have been far-reaching and there has been criticism of teachers for not carrying out adequately what society expects of them. New Zealand and England have offices of inspection, and evaluate schools regularly; the federal nature of the USA makes generalisation more difficult, but evaluation is usually carried out by school districts.

In Spain, schools and teachers are seen as important agents in society. A more collaborative approach to inspection is adopted where inspectors both advise groups of schools and form part of the team when formal inspections are carried out. A partnership approach is also a feature of school inspections in South Australia, where teachers are seconded to the review teams and there is parental, community, professional and pupil involvement in the inspection process. Schools are involved in the choice of inspection areas on the basis that 'the purpose of school reviews is to improve the schools involved' (Ofsted, 1993, pp. 10–12).

These analyses, together with the models of evaluation relationships set out earlier, are offered to help you to analyse the type of inspection regime in operation in your country and in your phase of education. You can read more about inspection in Brian Fidler's chapter 'External evaluation and inspection', in Bush and Bell (2002).

⊚ Reading

For further consideration of the evaluation process, please read Ann Briggs' chapter, 'The evaluation of learning', Chapter 11 in Bush, T. and Bell, L. (2002) *The Principles and Practice of Educational Management*.

This chapter questions whether learning itself can be evaluated but examines issues of equity in provision, together with ways in which departments and institutions can improve their effectiveness through evaluation. As you read, consider how your school or college uses evaluation processes to enable institutional improvement, a concept that will be discussed in the following section of this chapter.

❑ **Key learning points**

- Planning is a concept that takes place at institutional, course, class and individual level. It is a process complemented and completed by the activities of monitoring and evaluation.

- Programmes of assessment are most meaningful for the learner when the assessment criteria are fully shared and there is a coherent framework of assessment throughout the institution.

- Purposeful monitoring is an essential part of the evaluation process.

- Evaluation – making a judgement on either the curriculum 'process' or 'product' – is the way in which an institution can learn developmentally about itself. Its success depends upon the choice of appropriate criteria, the involvement of teachers and learners and the application of what has been learned.

Managing change for effective learning and teaching

> Real change . . . whether desired or not, represents a serious personal and collective experience charac-
> terised by ambivalence and uncertainty; and if the change works out it can result in a sense of mastery,
> accomplishment and professional growth (Fullan, 1991, p. 33).

The final section of this book deals with the most difficult task for the educational manager: managing change. As the quotation above indicates, change, however necessary or welcome it may be, is
also potentially threatening as it disturbs our equilibrium and forces us to think and act in unaccus-
tomed ways. It may seriously challenge our deeply held beliefs about education and about how to
meet the needs of the learner. An understanding of the processes of planning, monitoring and evaluation, as discussed in the last section, is a valuable attribute in managing change with a sense of
'accomplishment and professional growth'. Without these skills, change, once initiated, cannot be
embedded. But to understand the process we need to start further back to consider what initiates
change in educational institutions.

Change can be:

- Externally imposed

- Undertaken in response to external factors: markets, stakeholder needs, national curriculum demands

- Collaboratively devised (e.g. in partnership with local or regional education departments/employ-
ers/partner schools)

- Internally generated ('top down', 'bottom up' or an integration of both).

You will no doubt be able to identify in your own institution examples of some, if not all, of these
changes. These could be as follows:

- Institutional response to national curriculum changes or to variations in external student assessment frameworks.

- Changes in vocational curricula in response to developments in professional, business or manufacturing practice.

- Collaborative approaches by 'clusters' of primary, secondary and tertiary institutions (for example,
to provision for students with disabilities or to social needs within the area).

- Management restructuring to enable more effective school or college operation.

- Teacher-led initiatives (for example, to extend the use of ICT in the curriculum).

In relation to the management of learning and teaching, the changes could be in the goals set for the
teaching programme or for the institution as a whole; in the skills required of the managers, staff or
students; or in the philosophy, beliefs or behaviour of the school or college community – and often all
three of these areas are involved.

It is no wonder effective change is difficult to achieve and that the management of change offers fertile
ground for research and writing!

Change as a management concept

The most influential writer of recent years on the management of change in education is Michael Fullan, as quoted above. In a series of books and articles he has mapped out frameworks for understanding and implementing change. He writes with four main objectives:

1. To make curriculum change processes explicit and visible

2. To identify factors relating to achieving success in delivering the curriculum

3. To develop insights into the nature of change as a process

4. To develop appropriate action programmes in the light of acquired knowledge (Fullan, 1989, p. 144).

Linking school and curriculum management, Fullan (1993, pp. 9–19) offers a four-dimensional model:

1. Theories of education – what we ought to be doing in schools and colleges

2. Theories of organisation – how we should organise in order to achieve

3. Theories of change – what causes progress towards where we want to be

4. Theories of changing – what has to be done to influence these causes.

These four theories, says Fullan, are like the edges of a billiard table, setting boundaries, absorbing and transmitting energy. He points out that any transition devours energy as it involves new uses of resources, changing practices or behaviours and altering beliefs and understanding. Too little change can be just as stressful as too much as the institution or the individual gradually ceases to be stimulated to perform well. Successful change involves *ownership* of the processes by those involved in them. This last concept is developed further in his more recent work (1999).

Fullan states we need to consider the following when addressing change:

The soundness of proposed changes: not all change proposals are 'authentic'; they may have been made for a variety of reasons. Also, if change is as profoundly disturbing as it appears to be, then there is little chance of all proposed changes being implemented.

Understanding the failure of well intentioned change: new policies may be sincerely hoped for and adopted naively without the adopters realising their implications, or understanding the specific changes needed for implementation.

Guidelines for understanding the nature and feasibility of particular changes: analysis through what Fullan terms the 'objective dimension' is needed to assess the feasibility of changes. For curriculum change, this would mean checking the goals, beliefs and teaching strategies involved in the change were mutually consistent and coherent, clearly understood and achievable.

The realities of the status quo: change managers must understand what are the existing realities for all the people involved in order to assess the feasibility of the proposed change. The status quo may be so fixed there is little room for change.

The deepness of the change: change can strike at the core of the learned skills and beliefs of educators, creating doubts about their sense of competence and purpose. Changes that seem simple to the initiator may raise deep uncertainty in those who are not familiar with what is proposed.

The question of valuing: how do we know if a particular change is valuable, and who decides? (adapted from Fullan, 1991, pp. 43–44).

If change is so difficult to achieve successfully, how are we as managers to address it? A synthesis of Fullan's work, published in Lofthouse *et al.* (1995), presents key determinants of successful change:

1. *Professional development* Ongoing, interactive, cumulative.

2. *Active support of head/principal and senior managers* Encouraging, reinforcing, finding time, providing administrative support, applying positive pressure, managing boundaries, incorporating.

3. *Organisational climate* Explicit norms and values, creative and collegial climate, the school/college as a social institution.

It is interesting to note that Fullan puts in first place personal professional development. Where individual members of staff are accustomed to self-reflection and addressing their own professional needs through development activities, personal growth is encouraged. Collectively, this contributes to a climate in which institutional growth can also be achieved. As Fullan and Hargreaves (1992, p. 6) write: 'Teacher development is thus tantamount to transforming educational institutions.'

The set of characteristics presented above bears a close relationship to some of the factors seen as promoting institutional effectiveness discussed in Chapter 2 of this book, for example: 'firm, purposeful leadership'; the head as 'the leading professional'; 'collegiality and co-operation'; 'consistency of practice'; 'school-based staff development'. A college or school that can manage change appropriately is one that will have a good chance of being effective.

The activity that follows takes our thinking from the institutional level down to the level of the individual. A changing college or school will need managers with particular skills and attributes. You can use the activity on page 108 to assess your own capacity for change, and you could adapt it to assess the strengths and needs of colleagues.

❑ Our comments

We have no neat 'key' to your score to tell you that you are manager of the year or, alternatively, whether you should be reconsidering your career in education. It is not as simple as that.

Review the patterns of your ticked responses and use the numerical indicators as a checking mechanism for how you scored within sections. Review your overall profile. Most profiles echo the sentiments scattered over school reports: 'Could do better', 'Room for improvement.' If this is so, consider where improvement is needed and how it might be achieved. Do your results suggest some priorities for staff development?

Could you share the information generated by this profile with anyone at your present institution? Could you adapt it to help colleagues to assess their strengths and needs? Answering those questions will tell you something about the prevailing culture of your school or college.

Activity

Are you a successful change manager?

The following competency profile is a synthesis of work from Fullan and Hargreaves (1992) and Everard and Morris (1996) concerning qualities of successful change managers. The profile is divided into three sections: *knowledge, skills* and *personal characteristics*. Assess your own qualities as a manager of change, using the five-point scale.

Qualities of successful change managers

Very good	Good	Satisfactory	Unsatisfactory	Very weak
5	4	3	2	1

Knowledge of:

Rating

1. what motivates teachers
2. what makes schools/colleges successful organisations
3. the external pressures upon the institution
4. the leadership style of the headteacher or principal
5. your own management style
6. management techniques such as decision-making
7. the process of change
8. learning styles and training methods
9. staff development policies

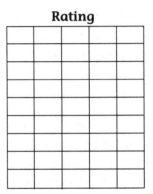

Skills in:

1. analysing complex social processes
2. converting theory into practice
3. setting objectives and planning their implementation
4. managing meetings
5. reconciling conflict
6. empathy
7. understanding micro-politics
8. public relations
9. counselling and interpersonal relations
10. training and teaching adults

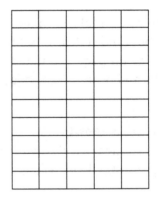

Personal characteristics:

1. consistent patterns of behaviour
2. an intellectual overview
3. positive and optimistic outlook
4. minimal need for recognition
5. willingness to take risks
6. ability to cope with personal stress
7. a calm approach
8. a high degree of self-knowledge
9. ability to tolerate ambiguity
10. highly developed listening skills

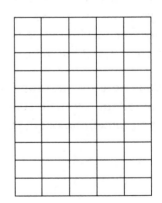

The intelligent school or college

How do we assess whether a college or school will be able to change successfully? MacGilchrist *et al.* (1997, pp. 104–109) take Gardner's concept of multiple intelligences, which we discussed in Chapter 2, and apply it to schools as institutions. They propose that the 'nine intelligences' they have constructed are characteristics that enable schools to address 'the core business of learning, teaching, effectiveness and improvement'. Here we take the 'intelligences' proposed by MacGilchrist *et al.*, and apply them to both colleges and schools in order to understand their relevance to the management of change.

❑ *Contextual intelligence*

This is 'the capacity of a school [or college] to see itself in relation to its wider community and the world of which it is a part' (MacGilchrist *et al.*, 1997, p. 104). It includes the capacity for *self-organisation*: the institution's 'ability to respond, think and act in ways that meet the varied requirements of its context, both internal and external' (MacGilchrist *et al.*, 1997, p. 105). In relation to change, this intelligence would enable the institution appropriately to assess its response to external and internal drivers for change and to understand the impact of institutional change upon the external environment.

❑ *Strategic intelligence*

'Strategic intelligence is about responding appropriately to the present, creating the future and anticipating the consequences' (MacGilchrist *et al.*, 1997, p. 106). It includes the capacity to communicate goals clearly and depends upon shared *ownership* of the proposed initiative: the aims and purposes of the proposed change need to be understood and shared by everyone.

❑ *Academic intelligence*

This intelligence values and promotes pupil and student engagement with learning: in these institutions the learners really matter. Likewise, teachers' learning is valued and promoted: the staff development so highly regarded by Fullan (1989) comes to the fore. In terms of managing change for effective learning and teaching, this capacity will enable staff to evaluate the benefits of the change for the learner and to assess what learning they will need to undertake themselves in order to achieve it.

❑ *Reflective intelligence*

The intelligent school or college 'is comfortable and skilled in its ability to interpret and use information and put it to the service of its [learners] and the organisation as a whole' (MacGilchrist *et al.*, 1997, p. 107). This enables the institution to monitor, reflect upon and evaluate the developments it undertakes.

❑ *Pedagogical intelligence*

This 'is characterised by the school [or college] seeing itself as a learning organisation: learning about learning . . . Learning and teaching are being regularly examined and developed: they are never an orthodoxy that remains unexamined' (MacGilchrist *et al.*, 1997, p. 107). It is easy to see that in a college or school with this characteristic, curriculum change would not be an 'event' but a continuous developmental process aided by the reflective intelligence described above.

❑ *Collegial intelligence*

Collegial intelligence is the capacity for staff, in particular, to work together to improve practice in the classroom. It recognises the added benefit of individuals improving and developing *together* and enables teachers to be key agents for change. 'Bottom up' changes, instigated by the classroom teachers themselves, would be empowered through collegial intelligence.

❏ *Emotional intelligence*

Goleman (1996, p. 34) proposes that possessing emotional intelligence is vital for learning to take place. On an institutional level, it concerns the capacity of the school or college 'to allow the feelings of both [learners] and staff to be owned, expressed and respected' (MacGilchrist *et al.*, 1997 p. 108). It is a capacity that will be needed in addressing Fullan's (1991) concern about the deepness of change: emotional intelligence would enable staff better to understand the potential and actual effects of change upon others.

❏ *Spiritual intelligence*

'Spiritual intelligence is characterised by a fundamental valuing of the lives and development of all members of a school [or college] community: that they all matter and have something to contribute' (MacGilchrist *et al.*, 1997, p. 109). It is this type of intelligence that may enable us to assess Fullan's 'question of valuing' (1991, p. 44) in relation to change. Sometimes change, particularly that imposed from the outside, seems to run counter to what our spiritual intelligence tells us: spiritual intelligence should keep us in touch with the true worth of the learners and teachers within the community, and may serve to mitigate the effects of seemingly 'unfeeling' change.

❏ *Ethical intelligence*

Ethical intelligence 'is characterised by a concern to ensure access for all [learners] to a broad and balanced curriculum and a concern about the distribution and use of resources' (MacGilchrist *et al.*, 1997, p. 109). Within a change context, it will enable staff to ask questions about the equity of proposed changes, for both learners and staff.

👁 Reading

Please read the chapter by Hugh Busher, 'Managing change to improve learning', Chapter 17 in Bush, T. and Bell, L. (2002) *The Principles and Practice of Educational Management*.

As you read, note his analysis of the contexts of change and the roles of leaders in bringing it about. What do you learn from this chapter that relates to your own institution?

❏ **Our comments**

Your response will depend upon your own context and on whether change for your institution is largely something imposed from the outside or proposed from the inside. You will have noticed from the chapter how management of change depends upon the cultures of the school or college, and you may like to think about what influence your own institutional culture would have. Busher is concerned especially with the personal agency of senior and middle leaders in bringing about change and sees a strong role for middle manager here, particularly in working with staff development to bring about change. For Busher, teachers are transformational leaders – is that so in your case?

Bearing in mind the contexts for change discussed in the reading above, in the next section we take the process of change further, looking at issues concerning the implementation of change for effective learning and teaching.

Conditions for implementing change

First, let us consider an example from the UK further education sector. In writing about achieving whole-college change, Flint (1994, p. 63) introduces the concept of congruence, an idea developed by a colleague of his, Angela Myers. Her thoughts are portrayed through the medium of congruent triangles. Only one of her three triangles is presented here (Figure 3.9): that which represents the institution open to change. Flint acknowledges his college has yet to achieve congruence on all the various points of the triangle portrayed here. He stresses the value of the model as a vehicle for debate 'amongst those interested enough to take part' about the future of the college, and for the achievement of a 'critical mass' of staff willing to accept the concept of challenge and change.

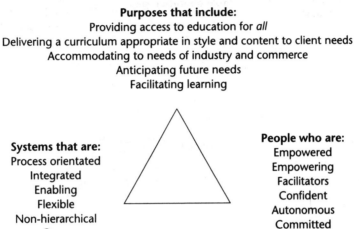

Figure 3.9 Characteristics of an institution open to change
Source: Flint (1994, p. 63) after Myers

Activity

Values underpinning change

In the institution and the national culture within which you work, you and your colleagues may have different values you feel would underpin successful development and change. Try to devise your own triangle, preferably through debate with colleagues, as to what the characteristics of the ideal *purposes*, *systems* and *people* would be.

❑ Our comments

One interesting aspect of this activity is the degree to which you were able to share it with colleagues. Are your colleagues interested in change or are they weary of it? Do they wish they had more chance to initiate and achieve it? How different was your list from that of the one portrayed? Why do you think it was different?

Flint commented that not all characteristics were in place in his college, and the list is best discussed as an 'ideal type'. Given the difficulties surrounding change activities and the acceptance that ideal conditions are unlikely to exist, change agents often come up against what is termed the *implementation gap*. Here the change is planned, and seeming acceptance and understanding is achieved, but the change is not fully implemented and embedded. This situation is represented diagrammatically by Cowham (1996) – seen here in Figure 3.10 – when illustrating the development of quality systems at his further education college.

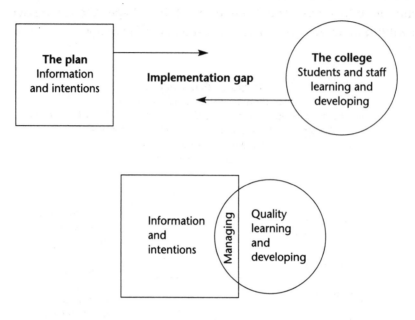

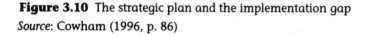

Figure 3.10 The strategic plan and the implementation gap
Source: Cowham (1996, p. 86)

Cowham highlights the activity of *managing* as crucial to closing the implementation gap. Implementing the large-scale change his college was undertaking involved three working groups, each led by a member of the SMT who worked to 'translate' the strategic plan into operating statements. They also reported back to a 'strategic group' their proposed amendments to the strategic plan, based on their discussions. The strategic group amended the original plan as necessary and worked on structures for action planning and review of the developments. Cowham reports a high level of participation in the planning process that, together with the provision for review, helped to bridge the implementation gap and embed the reform.

Not all implementation will involve such a lengthy process and such a level of detail as has been described above, but the example serves to illustrate Fullan's caveat about well intentioned reform that fails to take place. The first important factor is to achieve sufficient understanding and ownership of the reform on the part of all who are to implement it. Where open discussion can take place and amendments can be proposed, the implementation process will stand a greater chance of success but, in the case of externally imposed changes, the main thrust of the discussion is likely to be how the change can be accommodated within the current philosophy and practices of the institution. Where the underpinning philosophy and the basic framework of practice are threatened, there may be only token compliance.

The second important factor in bridging the implementation gap is the setting up of effective monitoring and review processes, as described earlier in this chapter. If these are not present, all the effort and energy of the change may be wasted. Not only do systems of monitoring and review help to ensure the development is still happening after the initial implementation phase, but their presence also helps to acknowledge that the reform may not have been 'right first time' and offers regular opportunities for adjustment and reassessment.

Managing small-scale change

Much of the foregoing discussion has implied that change will take place on a macro level, instigated by a national government, a senior management team or an influential group of teachers. As the statements about the importance of staff development and the whole staff being involved in learning imply, many changes will be undertaken and achieved on a very small scale. Indeed, it could be argued a college or school that is constantly carrying through successful small changes will be best prepared for the bigger ones.

In their book *Practitioner Research in Education: Making a Difference*, Middlewood *et al.* (1999) investigate the effect of small-scale research projects on schools and colleges. The examples selected here concern changes directly affecting learning and teaching: to appreciate the breadth of projects undertaken and to gain insight into your own small-scale research activities, you would be well advised to read the whole book!

One of the researchers interviewed compared his school's accustomed practice for effecting change – a working party – with the activity of undertaking individual research:

> We set up a group of teachers, volunteers, enthusiastic mostly, who were interested. Our first meeting was good – lots of discussion and generally good thoughts about this issue. Second meeting, several people couldn't make it, so others lost heart. Third meeting we were still keen and thought it had been helpful to us individually. Eventually it faded away. We didn't have a clear focus, didn't set ourselves a clear brief or seek one. We didn't have accountability and so on. My own research assignment into pupil motivation was limited but I learned a lot more which I can apply in my own teaching and possibly in the department (Julian, Corby school, cited in Middlewood *et al.*, 1999, p. 122).

Interestingly, Julian does not condemn the notion of working parties; instead he analyses the missing elements that might have helped this one to achieve – a clear focus, a brief, accountability.

Some of the researchers interviewed reported their findings were contrary to their expectations: interestingly, in many cases the school or college was found to be functioning well – or as well as its 'neighbours' – in areas where the researcher thought it was deficient. This reminds us of two of Fullan's caveats: of testing the soundness of proposed changes and of understanding the failure of well intentioned changes. If in these cases change had been embarked upon without the research being undertaken, it might have proved unnecessary and disturbing.

One research project, carried out by Mel in a Northamptonshire school, concerned the issue of homework. The parents at Mel's school were encouraged to work in partnership with the school to ensure homework was done properly: they signed a 'homework diary' at regular intervals to say work had been done. On investigating the two key partners in the agreement – the students and the parents – Mel found the following:

- Parents were not clear what their part was in the partnership involved in homework (the signature in the diary was done dutifully but had little meaning for parents).
- Parents simply did not know how they could best help their children.
- Students were not clear about the purpose of homework. Although the purposes were printed in the diary, most students admitted they did not read this part and it did not link with the work they were given to do.

Moreover, in examining the feedback given by the teachers on the students' homework, Mel deduced the teachers themselves might also be unclear about its purpose:

> The school prided itself upon its relationship with parents, yet here was a problem which it had not fully understood. However, as the relationship was genuine, and as staff at various levels in the school were keen to put the situation right, purposeful discussion ensued and a number of measures were introduced to increase student and parent understanding and involvement. Significantly, the school has a 'school improvement group' which will continue to monitor the situation as part of its brief (ibid., pp. 127–28).

Many of the pieces of research reported in Middlewood *et al.* were felt by the researcher concerned to have no lasting impact, other than on their own insight and practice. In schools or colleges where there was a group of researchers, the chances for whole-institution improvement were increased. Success also was enabled where the researcher – or other managers – had support in disseminating and embedding the proposed new practice, and where there was a strong desire to maintain the impetus of the improvement. Hopkins *et al.* (1994, p. 4) identify key activities at this stage of change management:

- An emphasis on embedding the change within the school's structure; its organisation and resources
- The elimination of competing or contradictory practices
- Strong and purposeful links to other change efforts
- Widespread use in the school
- An adequate bank of local facilitators.

Based upon the experiences of the researchers they surveyed, Middlewood and his colleagues (1999, p. 157) consider the following different levels of change may occur as a result of individual research:

1. *Small-scale change* – an individual undertakes a piece of research in an area where he or she has some jurisdiction and is therefore able to act, often in a quite practical way, to implement recommendations based on the findings. The outcome could be termed 'instrumental'.

2. *Potential long-term change* – research produces information which may impact on the individual researcher and on those to whom the research findings are disseminated. It is probable that such data may inform future action and may bring about 'conceptual effects'.

3. *Whole-school or college change* – the researcher has the active support of others in the school or college; the backing of senior management is particularly relevant. This may be as part of a whole-school initiative. Here the outcome is likely to be 'conceptual'.

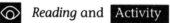 *Reading* and Activity

Successful change

Look again at the case studies presented in the chapter 'Managing the learning environment' by Ann Briggs, Chapter 11 in Middlewood, D. and Burton, N. (2001) *Managing the Curriculum*. They begin on page 182.

None of these changes arises directly out of research, although perhaps it is no coincidence all were undertaken by researchers. All, up to the date of writing, are being successfully implemented and embedded. From the information offered in the case studies, and from what you have read in the chapter so far, why do you think they are successful?

❏ **Our comments**

Given the number of tools for analysis provided in this chapter, your conclusions may differ from ours. Here are key features we think are important:

Booth Lower School

- The changes proposed are sound – the need for change is visible.
- Some disturbance was involved, but the benefits experienced served to minimise the anxiety.
- The changes were seen to be valuable, as classroom conditions for both learners and teachers were improved.
- A creative climate exists in the school, which is being fostered by these developments.

Leasowes Community College

- The changes were large but their feasibility was well explored and explained before implementation.
- Part of the development (that of the resource centres) is gradual – so it can be assessed.
- Staff are open to staff development.
- Senior staff took a strong role in encouraging and reinforcing.

Midlands Further Education College

- In considering Fullan's 'objective dimension':
  - the goals are specific;
  - the means of implementation are flexibly provided; and
  - the number of changes involved are great – but well facilitated.
- Staff are open to staff development.
- The status quo was found not to be fixed!

A systematic approach to change

So far we have explored some of the complexities presented by change management, tried to understand the skills and 'intelligences' needed to implement change successfully, considered how to bridge the implementation gap and how to use small-scale research in initiating change. To attempt a summary of what we have learned, we turn to Everard and Morris (1996), who present a 'systematic approach to change.' They propose (ibid., pp. 233–35) that six key stages have to be carried out sequentially:

1. A preliminary *diagnosis* or reconnaissance, leading to a *decision* to undertake a change programme: is the change sound? Is it inherently likely to succeed?

2. Determining the *future*: what do we want to happen? What will happen if we do nothing?

3. Characterising the *present*: what are we here for? What are the demands on us? What is stopping us? What is working for us?

4. Identifying the *gaps* between present and future to determine the work to be done to close them: who is resistant? Who can help the change? Who should manage it?

5. Managing the *transition* from present to future: who does what by when? How will we gain commitment?

6. Evaluating and monitoring the change: was success achieved/will the change endure? What has been learned?

Everard and Morris concede that their formula need not be followed slavishly and that other writers have presented formulae that may work equally well. They suggest that some elements of their sequence may need more attention than others, and that in the case of minor changes the processes should not be laboured, but they warn against missing out any elements completely.

Activity

Tracking the process of change

Think of any major initiative in your school or college that was linked to improving effective learning and teaching. Describe it in *any* ways you find helpful – e.g. by drawing a flow diagram, by noting or describing key meetings, by listing the major participants and describing them with key phrases.

Stage 1
Doing any or all of the above contributes to stage 1. 'Brainstorm' the event – do not worry at this stage about sequence. What do you remember, and why was it important to you?

Stage 2
Now begin to be more systematic in your interrogation of the evidence you are thinking of. Try to answer the following questions:

1. Where did the initiative come from? Was it external or internal or a combination of both?
2. When, where or from whom did you first learn of the initiative?
3. When and how (if at all) was the initiative first brought into the formal decision-making structures of your institution (e.g. staff or departmental meetings; memos, letters or minutes circulated?).
4. At this point (the formal initiation of the event) you may find it helpful to draw a diagram of who was involved in the project. What were their responsibilities and tasks? Who delegated what to whom and over what period?
5. Shift the time frame of the initiative forward to whenever you feel was the critical time in terms of 'major implementation'. At this point, make a list of all who were involved – and another list of those who should have been involved but were not. You may find it helpful to categorise people as follows:
   - People for the initiative – why?
   - People willing to let the initiative happen – why?
   - People generally against the initiative – why?
   - People determined to block the initiative – why?
6. Did the initiative survive long enough to be implemented? If it died – who or what killed it? If it survived, how was it implemented, by whom and with what results?
7. Is there still tangible evidence of the initiative having taken root? How clear and reliable is this evidence? What people and mechanisms sustain the initiative? If any were to be withdrawn, what would happen?
8. How does the initiative fit into the curriculum philosophy of your school or college? How does this affect the way the change was managed?
9. Has there been any review or evaluation of the initiative? If so when, and prompted by what?

Stage 3
You can now play the 'perfect change manager' with the benefit of hindsight! If you had been the senior manager tasked with the responsibility of implementing the initiative, how would you have gone about the exercise? Try to answer at least three critical points:

1. What would you have done the same?
2. What would you have done differently?
3. What would you not have done at all?

In your reflection, you may wish to note those things within your institution that are essential to success and those that are likely to bring about failure.

Note: This is a very long and complex activity and you may wish to use it as the basis for an assignment.

❑ Our comments

A review such as this can be a sobering experience. It can be a shock to find out how much time and energy were expended in achieving only a little and, sometimes, in achieving nothing at all. Moreover, a dispassionate review of any curriculum change underlines the problematic nature of change, especially the fact it can cause competent teachers and managers to feel temporary symptoms of insecurity and incompetence. When people feel threatened, insecure or anxious, they generally do not act in sensible or rational ways. It may be that your initiative was defeated by the 'fear factor' – if the initiative succeeded, it would be valuable to understand how the 'fear factor' was handled.

❑ Key learning points

- Change is a complex process that can be generated internally or externally to the institution.

- Theories of change, such as those proposed by Fullan, can help us to understand the complexities better.

- Research into change has enabled us to identify determinants of successful change and the skills needed by successful change managers.

- The consideration of the 'intelligences' possessed by a college or school can help to determine its fitness to achieve change.

- Change is often thwarted by the 'implementation gap'. Learning how best to manage to 'bridge the gap' is essential.

- Practitioner research can be a useful precursor to institutional change – but not all practitioner research leads to significant change.

- A systematic approach to change can help change managers to avoid some of the pitfalls associated with change management.

---

4. Conclusions: focus upon the learner

In this book we have encouraged readers to think broadly – across concepts, curricula and countries. We have considered how curricula are conceived and what factors influence their design. We have discussed how the processes of learning and teaching are understood in order to see how they may be managed, and looked at learning, both in the classroom and beyond, in order to see how teaching styles influence learners, and how learners may benefit from the various learning environments they inhabit. The roles of teachers and managers within educational settings have been addressed, specifically in Chapter 3, but also in the discussion throughout the book of the various contexts in which learning and teaching are managed. The processes of planning, monitoring and evaluation have been examined, together with the ever-present task of managing change.

Within this framework we have encouraged people working in one educational setting to consider models from other settings. This is not with the intention that ideas and practice from one national culture or from one phase of education should be transferred wholesale to another. It is rather that by considering other educational settings we may see our own more clearly and identify ways forward that will benefit our institutions and our learners.

Within the busy processes of managing schools and colleges, it is sometimes easy to become so absorbed in the processes of managing that, for a time, we lose sight of the purpose: the progress in learning and the personal growth of the learners within our care. It is therefore to the learners themselves that this book is dedicated and upon whom the final focus should fall.

Whether they are learning in large or small groups, in very basic accommodation or with the educational benefits financial resources and modern technology can bring, whether they are young, just embarking upon their life of learning or older 'returners' to the classroom or to workplace learning, the international research upon which we have drawn demonstrates systems that, at their best, focus upon the needs of these individual learners. The test of any one of the models and ideas we have presented is: how will this insight enable me and my institution to help our pupils and students to achieve? Each child and student arriving at the doors of his or her new school or college has his or her own expectations. These are largely based upon previous experience of education or what they have been told about the phase they are about to enter but, hopefully, the expectations include the wish to learn, to understand and to achieve. As teachers and managers we necessarily consider learners collectively – as members of class and course groups or, even more broadly, as members of the whole school or college. In most teaching settings we plan for learners' needs as members of classes, cohorts and groups. But the learning we manage takes place on an individual basis, inside the mind of each child and adult learner.

We hope this book will enable you to manage learning and teaching in ways that enable you to focus on the learner. Within the school or college setting, their needs are remarkably similar to those of their teachers. As Phelan and her colleagues (1992, p. 704) report:

> Teachers want to be respected, and want to work with students who care; who exhibit humour, openness and consideration; and who are actively involved in subject-area content. Furthermore teachers want to be in safe and tension-free environments.

> Students say they want the same thing from their teachers and schools.

References

Adam, E. (1987) Steps to success; the principal's role. Burlington, Ontario: Halton Board of Education, unpublished manuscript.

Adult Learning Australia (ALA) (2001) www.ala.asn.au/about/directions2001.html (online October 2001).

Aedo-Richmond, R. and Richmond, M. (1999) Recent curriculum change in post-Pinochet Chile. In B. Moon and P. Murphy (eds.) *Curriculum in Context*. London: Paul Chapman.

Ainley, P. and Bailey, B. (1997) *The Business of Learning*. London: Cassell.

Alden, J. (1998) *A Trainer's Guide to Web-based Instruction: Getting Started on Intranet- and Internet-Based Training*. Alexandria, VA: American Society for Training and Development.

Alexander, R. (2001) *Culture and Pedagogy*. Oxford: Blackwell.

Alexander, R., Rose, J. and Woodhead, C. (1992) *Curriculum Organisation and Classroom Practice in Primary Schools: A Discussion Paper*. London: Department of Education and Science.

Al Tobi, K. (2001) Selection of students in Sultan Qaboos institutes for Islamic sciences. Unpublished MBA in educational management dissertation, University of Leicester.

American Association for Adult and Continuing Education (AAACE) (2001) www.aaace.org/general.html (online October 2001).

Aristotle (undated) *Politics. Book 8*. London: Folio Classical Library.

Aspinwall, K., Simkins, T., Wilkinson, J. and McCauley, H. (1992) *Managing Evaluation in Education*. London: Routledge.

Atkin, J. (1996) Values and beliefs about learning: principles and practice. *IARTV Seminar Series*, May, no. 54.

Atkin, J. (1999) Learning to know. Paper presented at Victorian Principals' conference, 'Values for a learning community', 15–17 August.

Atkinson, J.W. (1964) *An Introduction to Motivation*. New York: Van Nostrand.

Baddely, G. (1991) Teachers and learners. In D. Hustler *et al.* (eds.) *Learning Environments for the Whole Curriculum*. London: Unwin Hyman.

Banathy, B.H. (1993) Comprehensive systems design in education: designing education around the learning experience level. *Education Technology* 33(3): 33–35.

Beare, H. (1997) Designing a break-the-mould school for the future. Paper presented at the virtual conference of the Australian Council for Educational Administration.

Beare, H., Caldwell, B.J. and Millikan, R.H. (1989) *Creating an Excellent School*. London: Routledge.

Becher, T. (1989) The National Curriculum and the implementation gap. In M. Preedy (ed.) *Approaches to Curriculum Management*. Milton Keynes: Open University Press.

Becher, T. and Kogan, M. (1992) *Process and Structure in Higher Education* (2nd edn). London: Routledge.

Belbin, M. (1981) *Management Teams: Why They Succeed or Fail*. London: Heinemann.

Bell, D. and Ritchie, R. (1999) *Towards Effective Subject Leadership in the Primary School*. Buckingham: Open University Press.

Bennett, N. (1995) *Managing Professional Teachers: Middle Management in Primary and Secondary Schools*. London: Paul Chapman.

Bentley, T. (1998) *Learning Beyond the Classroom: Education for a Changing World*. London: Routledge.

Bernstein, B. (1971) On the classification and framing of educational knowledge. In M.F.P. Young (ed.) *Knowledge and Control*. New York: Collier-Macmillan.

Betts, M. and Smith, R. (1998) *Developing the Credit-Based Modular Curriculum in Higher Education*. London: Falmer Press.

Bikson, T.K. and Eveland, J.D. (1990) The interplay of work group structure and computer support. In J. Galegher *et al.* (eds.) *Intellectual Teamwork: Social and Technological Foundations of Cooperative Work*. Hillsdale, NJ: Lawrence Erlbaum Associates.

Blandford, S. (1997) *Middle Management in Schools.* London: Pitman.

Bolam, R., McMahon, A., Pocklington, K. and Weindling, D. (1993) *Effective Management in Schools.* London: HMSO.

Bottery, M. (1992) *The Ethics of Educational Management.* London: Cassell.

Briggs, A.R.J. (1999) Promoting learning style analysis among vocational students. *Education and Training* 42(1): 16–23.

Briggs, A.R.J. (2001a) Managing the learning environment. In D. Middlewood and N. Burton (eds.) *Managing the Curriculum.* London: Paul Chapman.

Briggs, A.R.J. (2001b) Academic middle managers in further education: reflections on leadership. *Research in Post-Compulsory Education* 6(2): 223–36.

Briggs, A.R.J. (2002) Monitoring and evaluating learning. In T. Bush and L. Bell (eds.) *Principles and Practice of Educational Management.* London: Paul Chapman.

Burton, N. (2001) Managing the planning of learning and teaching. In D. Middlewood and N. Burton (eds.) *Managing the Curriculum.* London: Paul Chapman.

Burton, N., Middlewood, D. with Blatchford, R. (2001) Models of curriculum organisation. In D. Middlewood and N. Burton (eds.) *Managing the Curriculum.* London: Paul Chapman.

Bush, T. and Bell, L. (eds.) (2002) *The Principles and Practice of Educational Management.* London: Paul Chapman.

Bush, T. and Coleman, M. (2000) *Leadership and Strategic Management in Education.* London: Paul Chapman.

Bush, T. and West-Burnham, J. (eds.) (1994) *The Principles of Educational Management.* Harlow: Longman.

Bush, T., Coleman, M. and Si, X. (1998) Managing secondary schools in China. *Compare* 28(2): 183–95.

Byatt, J. and Davies, K. (1998) *The RSA Study Guide.* Coventry: RSA.

Caldwell, B.J. and Spinks, J.M. (1992) *Leading the Self-Managing School.* London: Falmer Press.

Centre for Educational Research and Innovation (CERI) (1995) *Schools under Scrutiny: Strategies for the Evaluation of School Performance.* Paris: OECD.

Chong, K.C. and Leong, W.F. (2000) *Singapore Schooling in the 21st Century* www.eddirect.com/associations/acea/conference/VC/aceavirt/chong.html (online October 2001).

Clarke, P. (2000) *Learning Schools, Learning Systems.* London: Continuum.

Coleman, M. (1999) Working with employers and business. In J. Lumby and N. Foskett (eds.) *Managing External Relations in Schools and Colleges.* London: Paul Chapman.

Coleman, M. and Briggs, A.R.J. (2000) Management of buildings and space. In M. Coleman and L. Anderson (eds.) *Managing Finance and Resources in Education.* London: Paul Chapman.

Coulby, D. (2000) *Beyond the National Curriculum: Cultural Centralism and Cultural Diversity in Europe and the USA.* London and New York: Routledge Falmer.

Cowham, T. (1996) Quality, chaos and the management of change in further education. In J. Bell and B. Harrison (eds.) *Vision and Values in Managing Education.* London: David Fulton.

Creemers, B.P.M and Reezigt, G.J. (1999) The role of school and classroom climate in elementary school learning environments. In H.J. Freiberg (ed.) *School Climate: Measuring, Improving and Sustaining Healthy Learning Environments.* London: Falmer Press.

Crombie White, R. (1997) *Curriculum Innovation: A Celebration of Classroom Practice.* Buckingham: Open University Press.

Croner (2000) *Croner's Head Teacher's Briefing* (Issue 185, 6 June).

Cumming, J. and Carbine, B. (1997) *Reforming Schools through Workplace Learning.* New South Wales: National Schools Network.

Dale, J.D. (1997) The new American school system: a learning organisation? *International Journal of Educational Reform* 6(1): 34–39.

Datta, C.J. (1994) The effects of cross-ethnic tutoring on interracial relationships and academic achievements. In B.R. Singh (ed.) *Improving Gender and Ethnic Relations: Strategies for Schools and Further Education.* London: Cassell.

Davies, B. and Ellison, L. (1999) *Strategic Direction and Development of the School*. London: Routledge.

Deal, T.E. (1985) The symbolism of effective schools. *The Elementary School Journal* 85(5): 601–20.

Deal, T.E. (1988) The symbolism of effective schools. In A. Westoby (ed.) *Culture and Power in Educational Organisations*. Milton Keynes: Open University Press.

DfEE (1998) *The Learning Age*. London: HMSO.

DfE/Ofsted (1995) *Governing Bodies and Effective Schools*. London: Department for Education.

DfEE (2000) *Research into Teacher Effectiveness: A Model of Teacher Effectiveness* (report by Hay McBer to the Department for Education and Employment, June) (www.dfes.gov.uk/teachingreforms/leadership/mcber/index.shtml) (online October 2001).

Dimmock, C. (1995) Restructuring for school effectiveness: leading, organising and teaching for effective learning. *Educational Management and Administration* 23(1): 5–18.

Dimmock, C. (1998) Restructuring Hong Kong's schools: the applicability of western theories, policies and practices to an Asian culture. *Journal of the British Educational Management and Administration Society* 26(4): 363–77.

Dimmock, C. (2000) *Designing the Learning Centred School: A Cross-Cultural Perspective*. London: Falmer Press.

Duffy, M. (1988) *The School Curriculum: School Management in Practice*. Harlow: Longman.

Earley, P. (1998) Middle management – the key to organisational success? In D. Middlewood and J. Lumby (eds.) *Strategic Management in Schools and Colleges*. London: Paul Chapman.

Edwards, D. and Mercer, N. (1981) *Common Knowledge: The Development of Understanding in the Classroom*. London: Routledge.

Engestrom, Y. (2001) *Training for Change: New Approach to Instruction and Learning in Working Life*. Geneva: International Labour Office.

Epstein, D. (1998) *Failing Boys?* Buckingham: Open University Press.

Epstein, J.L. (1995) School/family partnerships: caring for the children we share. *Phi Delta Kappan* 76(9): 701–12.

Eraut, M., Alderton, J., Cole, G. and Senker, P. (1998) Learning from other people at work. In F. Coffield (ed.) *Learning at Work*. Bristol: The Policy Press.

European Association for the Education of Adults (EAEA) (2001) www.eaea.org/doc.meopol.html (online October 2001).

European Council (2000), Presidency conclusions.

Everard, K.B. and Morris, G. (1996) *Effective School Management* (3rd edn). London: Paul Chapman.

Fazey, D. (1996) Guidance for learner autonomy. In S. McNair (ed.) *Putting Learners at the Centre*. Sheffield: DfEE.

Fidler, B. (1989) Staff appraisal – theory, concepts and experience in other organizations and problems of adaptation to education. In C. Riches and C. Morgan (eds.) *Human Resource Management in Education*. Milton Keynes: Open University Press.

Fidler, B. (1997) Organisational structure and organisational effectiveness. In A. Harris *et al.* (eds.) *Organisational Effectiveness and Improvement in Education*. Buckingham: Open University Press.

Flint, C. (1994) A modest revolution. In S. Weil (ed.) *Introducing Change from the Top in Universities and Colleges*. London: Kogan Page.

Fouts, J.T. and Chan, C.K. (1997) The development of work-study and school enterprises in China's schools. *Journal of Curriculum Studies* 29(1): 31–46.

Fraser, B.J. (1999) Using learning environment assessments to improve classroom and school climates. In H.J. Freiberg (ed.) *School Climate: Measuring, Improving and Sustaining Healthy Learning Environments*. London: Falmer Press.

Freiberg, H.J. and Stein, T.A. (1999) Measuring, improving and sustaining healthy learning environments. In H.J. Freiberg (ed.) *School Climate: Measuring, Improving and Sustaining Healthy Learning Environments*. London: Falmer Press.

Fullan, M. (1989) Managing curriculum change. In M. Preedy (ed.) *Approaches to Curriculum Management*. Buckingham: Open University Press.

Fullan, M. (1991) *The New Meaning of Educational Change*. London: Cassell.

Fullan, M. (1993) *Change Forces: Probing the Depths of Educational Reform*. London: Falmer Press

Fullan, M. (1999) *Change Forces: The Sequel.* London: Falmer Press.

Fullan, M. and Hargreaves, A. (1992) *Teacher Development and Educational Change.* London: Falmer Press.

Fuller, A. and Unwin, L. (2002) Developing pedagogies for the changing workplace. In K. Evans *et al.* (eds.) *Working to Learn: Transforming Learning in the Workplace.* London: Kogan Page.

Further Education National Training Organisation (2000) *National Occupational Standards for Management in Further Education* (draft 7). London: FENTO.

Gaine, C. and George, R. (1999) *Gender, 'Race' and Class in Schooling: A New Introduction.* London: Falmer Press.

Gardner, H. (1983) *Frames of Mind.* London: Fontana.

Gibbs, G., Rust, C., Jenkins, A. and Jaques, D. (1994) *Developing Students' Transferable Skills.* Oxford: Centre for Staff Development.

Gillborn, D. and Gipps, C. (1996) *Recent Research on the Achievements of Ethnic Minority Pupils.* London: Ofsted/HMSO.

Glasser, W. (2000) *Every Student can Succeed.* Chatsworth, CA: William Glasser Inc.

Goddard, D. and Clinton, B. (1994) Learning networks. In S. Ranson and J. Tomlinson (eds.) *School Cooperation: New Forms of Local Governance.* Harlow: Longman

Goleman, D. (1995) *Emotional Intelligence: Why it can Matter more than IQ.* London: Bloomsbury.

Gomes, C. A. (1991) Vocational education financing: an example of participation by employers in Brazil. *Prospect* 21(3), 457–65.

Green, R. (1993) Business and education partnerships: a pre-school through higher education perspective in the United States. *Journal of Educational Finance* 19(4): 138–44.

Hancock, V. (1997) Creating the 'information age' school. *Educational Leadership* 55(3): 60–63.

Hardie, B. (2001) Managing monitoring of the curriculum. In D. Middlewood and N. Burton (eds.) *Managing the Curriculum.* London: Paul Chapman.

Hargreaves, D. (1984) *Improving London's Schools.* London: ILEA.

Helsby, G. (1999) *Changing Teachers' Work,* Buckingham: Open University Press.

Hillage, J., Hyndley, K. and Pike, G. (1995) *Employers' Views of Education–Business Links.* Brighton: Institute for Employment Studies.

Ho, D.Y.F. (1993) Relational orientation in Asian social psychology. In U. Kin and J.W. Berry (eds.) *Indigenous Psychologies.* Newbury Park, CA: Sage.

Hodkinson, P. (1994) Empowerment as an entitlement in the post-16 curriculum. *Journal of Curriculum Studies* 26(5): 491–508.

Hodkinson, P. and Issitt, M. (eds.) (1995) *The Challenge of Competence.* London: Cassell.

Holloway, S.D. (1988) Concepts of ability and effort in Japan and the US. *Review of Educational Research* 58: 327–45.

Honey, P. and Mumford, A. (1986) *The Manual of Learning Styles.* Maidenhead: Peter Honey.

Hopkins, D., Ainscow, M. and West, M. (1994) *School Improvement in an Era of Change.* London: Cassell.

International Council for Adult Education (2001) *The Ocho Rios Declaration: Adult Learning: A Key to Democratic Citizenship and Global Action* (www.web.net/icae.ordeceng.html) (online October 2001).

Jennings, Z. (1993) Innovations in Caribbean school systems: why some have become institutionalised and others have not. *Curriculum Studies* 2(3): 309–31.

Jin, L. and Cortazzi, M. (1998) Dimensions of dialogue: large classes in China. *International Journal of Educational Research* 29: 739–76.

Johansson, Y. (2000) *Chair's Conclusions of Rotterdam Conference on Schooling for Tomorrow* (OECD/CERI) (www.oecd.org/media/release/conclusionsrotterdam3November2000.htm) (online October 2001).

Joyce, B. and Showers, B. (1991) *Information Processing: Models of Teaching.* Aptos, CA: Booksend Laboratories.

Keefe, J.W. (1989) *Learning Style Profile Handbook. Volume 11. Developing Cognitive Skills.* Reston, VA: National Association of Secondary School Principals.

Kelly, A.V. (1999) *The Curriculum: Theory and Practice* (4th edn). London: Paul Chapman.

Kelly, A.V. (2000) *National Curriculum.* London: Paul Chapman.

Kolb, D.A. (1985) *A Learning Styles Inventory and Technical Manual.* Boston, MA: McBer.

Laurillard, D. (1993) *Rethinking University Teaching: A Framework for the Effective Use of Educational Technology*. London: Routledge.

Lave, J. and Wenger, E. (1991) *Situated Learning: Legitimate Peripheral Participation*. Cambridge: Cambridge University Press.

Lawton, D. (1983) *Curriculum Studies and Educational Planning*. London: Hodder & Stoughton.

Lawton, D. (1996) *Beyond the National Curriculum: Teacher Professionalism and Empowerment*. London: Hodder & Stoughton.

Lee, J.C.K. and Walker, A. (1997) Managing curriculum programmes and process: towards a whole-school approach. *Curriculum* 18(2): 97–105.

Lee, W.O. (1996) The cultural context of Chinese learners: conceptions of learning in the Confucian tradition. In D. Watkins and J. Biggs (eds.) *The Chinese Learner: Cultural, Psychological and Contextual Influences*. Hong Kong/Melbourne: Comparative Education Research Centre/Australian Council for Educational Research.

Leithwood, K., Jantzi, D. and Steinbach, R. (1999) *Changing Leadership for Changing Times*. Buckingham: Open University Press.

Le Métais, J. (1997) *Values and Aims in Curriculum and Assessment Frameworks*. London: School Curriculum and Assessment Authority (www.inca.org.uk/pdf/values_no_intro_97.pdf) (online October 2001).

Le Métais, J. (1998) Values and aims in curriculum and assessment frameworks: a 16-nation review. In B. Moon and P. Murphy (eds.) *Curriculum in Context*. London: Paul Chapman/Open University Press.

Le Métais, J. (1999b) *Legislating for Change: School Reforms in England and Wales, 1979–1994*. Slough: NFER.

Levin, B. (1994) Improving educational productivity: putting students at the center. *Phi Delta Kappan* 75(10): 758–60.

Lofthouse, M. (1992) *The Church Colleges, 1918–1939: The Struggle for Survival*. Research by: J. Billings & Co.

Lofthouse, M., Bush, T., Coleman, M., O'Neill, J., West-Burnham, J. and Glover, D. (1995) *Managing the Curriculum*. London: Financial Times/Pitman.

Loveless, A. (1995) *The Role of IT: Practical Issues for Primary Teachers*. London: Cassell.

Loveless, A (1998) *Where do You Stand to Get a Good View of Pedagogy? (*www.coe.uh.edu/insite.elec_pub/HTML1998/thlove.htlm) (online October 2001).

Lumby, J. (2001a) Framing teaching and learning in the twenty-first century. In D. Middlewood and N. Burton (eds.) *Managing the Curriculum*. London: Paul Chapman.

Lumby, J. (2001b) *Managing Further Education: Learning Enterprise*. London: Paul Chapman.

Lumby, J. and Foskett, N. (1999) *Managing external relations in schools and colleges*. London: Paul Chapman.

MacBeath, J. (1999) *Schools Must Speak for Themselves*. London: Routledge.

MacBeath, J. and Mortimore, P. (2001) *Improving School Effectiveness*. Buckingham: Open University Press.

Macbeth, A. (1993) Parent–teacher partnership: a minimum programme and a signed understanding. In M. Preedy (ed.) *Managing the Effective School*. London: Open University/Paul Chapman.

MacGilchrist, B., Myers, K. and Reed, J. (1997) *The Intelligent School*. London: Paul Chapman.

Marsden, C. (1989) Bridging the culture gap. In D. Warwick (ed.) *Linking Schools and Industry*. Oxford: Blackwell.

Martinez, P. and Munday, F. (1998) *9,000 Voices, Student Persistence and Dropout in Further Education*. London: FEFC.

McCarthy, B. (1990) Using the 4MAT system to bring learning styles to schools. *Educational Leadership* 48(2): 31–37.

McCormick, R. (1999) Curriculum development and new information technology. In B. Moon and P. Murphy (eds.) *Curriculum in Context*. London: Paul Chapman/Open University.

Middlewood, D. (2001) Leadership of the curriculum: setting the vision. In D. Middlewood and N. Burton (eds.) *Managing the Curriculum*. London: Paul Chapman.

Middlewood, D. and Burton, N. (eds.) (2001) *Managing the Curriculum*. London: Paul Chapman.

Middlewood, D., Coleman, M. and Lumby, J. (1999) *Practitioner Research in Education: Making a Difference.* London: Paul Chapman.

Muijs, D. and Reynolds, D. (2001) *Effective Teaching: Evidence and Practice.* London: Paul Chapman.

Murphy, M. (1994) Managing the use of space. In D. Warner and G. Kelly (eds.) *Managing Educational Property: A Handbook for Schools, Colleges and Universities.* Buckingham: Society for Research into Higher Education and Open University Press.

National Advisory Committee on Creative and Cultural Education (NACCCE) (1999) *All Our Futures: Creativity, Culture and Education.* Sudbury: DfEE Publications.

National Council of Teachers of Mathematics (USA) (2000) *Principles for Mathematics* (www.// standards.nctm.org/document/chapter2/equity.htm) (online October 2001).

Ofsted (1993) *Aspects of School Review in Southern Australia: A Report from the Office of Her Majesty's Chief Inspector of Schools.* London: HMSO.

O'Neill, J. (1994) Managing professional development. In T. Bush and J. West-Burnham (eds.) *The Principles of Educational Management.* Harlow: Longman.

Organisation for Economic Co-operation and Development (1973) *Styles of Curriculum Development.* Paris: OECD Publications.

Organisation for Economic Co-operation and Development (1994) *Teacher Quality: Synthesis of Country Studies.* Paris: OECD.

Organisation for Economic Co-operation and Development (1995) *Integrating Students with Special Needs in Schools.* Paris: OECD.

Owen, J. (1992) *Managing Education.* Harlow: Longman.

Owston, R.D. (1997) The World Wide Web: a technology to enhance teaching and learning. *Educational Research* 26(2): 27–33.

Phelan, P., Davidson, L. and Hanh, T.C. (1992) Speaking up: students' perspectives on school. *Phi Delta Kappan* 73(9): 695–704.

Preedy, M. (2001) Curriculum evaluation: measuring what we value. In D. Middlewood and N. Burton (eds.) *Managing the Curriculum.* London: Paul Chapman.

QCA/NFER (1998) *International Review of Curriculum and Assessment Frameworks: Thematic Studies (INCA)* (www.inca.org.uk) (online October 2001).

Queensland School Curriculum Council (2001) *Office of the Council – Equity* (www.qscc.qld.edu.au/ office/equity.html) (online October 2001).

Raggatt, P. and Williams, S. (2000) *Governments, Markets and Vocational Qualifications: An Anatomy of Policy.* London: Falmer Press.

Randle, K. and Brady, N. (1997) Managerialism and professionalism in the 'Cinderella' service. *Journal of Vocational Education and Training* 49(1): 121–358.

Reinert, H. (1976) One picture is worth a thousand words? Not necessarily! *The Modern Language Journal* 60: 160–68.

Reynolds, D. and Farrell, S. (1996) *Worlds Apart? A Review of International Surveys of Educational Achievement Involving England (OFSTED Reviews of Research).* London: HMSO.

Riding, R. (1991) *Cognitive Styles Analysis User Manual.* Birmingham: Learning and Training Technology.

Riding, R. and Raynor, S. (1999) *Cognitive Styles and Learning Strategies.* London: David Fulton.

Rogoff, B. and Chavajay, P. (1995) What's become of research on the cultural basis of cognitive development? *American Psychologist* 50(10): 859–77.

Rogoff, B., Mistry, J., Goncu, A. and Mosier, C. (1993) *Guided Participation in Cultural Activity by Toddlers and Caregivers. Monograph of the Society for Research into Child Development* 58.

Rosenthal, R. and Jacobson, L. (1968) *Pygmalion in the Classroom. Teacher Expectations and Pupils' Intellectual Growth.* New York: Holt, Reinhart & Winston.

Ross, A. (2000) *Curriculum Construction and Critique.* London: Falmer Press.

Salili, F. (1996) Accepting personal responsibility for learning. In D. Watkins and J. Biggs (eds.) *The Chinese Learner: Cultural, Psychological and Contextual Influences.* Hong Kong/Melbourne: Comparative Education Research Centre/Australian Council for Educational Research.

Salovey, P. and Mayer, J.D. (1990) Emotional intelligence. *Imagination, Cognition and Personality* 9: 185–211.

Sammons, P., Hillman, J. and Mortimore, P. (1995) *Key Characteristics of Effective Schools: A Review of School Effectiveness Research*. London: Ofsted.

Schein, E.H. (1985) *Organizational Culture and Leadership*. San Francisco, CA: Jossey-Bass.

Scott, P. (1989) Accountability, responsiveness and responsibility. In R. Glatter (ed.) *Educational Institutions and their Environments: Managing the Boundaries*. Milton Keynes: Open University Press.

Sergiovanni, T. (1984) Leadership and excellence in schools. *Educational Leadership* 41(5): 4–13.

Sergiovanni, T. (1989) Value-driven schools: the amoeba theory. In H. Walberg and S. Lane (eds.) *Organising for Learning: Towards the 21st Century*. Alexandria, VA: National Association of Secondary School Pupils.

Silcock, P. and Brundrett, M. (2001) The management consequences of different models of teaching and learning. In D. Middlewood and N. Burton (eds.) *Managing the Curriculum*. London: Paul Chapman.

Sommefeldt, D. (2001) Managing individual needs within an inclusive curriculum. In D. Middlewood and N. Burton (eds.) *Managing the Curriculum*. London: Paul Chapman.

Sorenson, J.S., Engelsgjerd, J., Francis, M., Miller, M. and Schuster, N. (1998) *The Gifted Program Handbook*. Palo Alto, CA: Dale Seymore.

Southworth, G. (1994) The learning school. In P. Ribbins and E. Burridge (eds.) *Improving Education: Promoting Quality in Schools*. London: Cassell.

Stahl, S.A. (1999) Different strokes for different folks? A critique of learning styles. *American Educator* 23(3): 27–31.

Stephenson, J. (1992) Capability and quality in higher education. In J. Stephenson (ed.) *Quality in Learning*. London: Kogan Page.

Stoll, L. and Fink, D. (1996) *Changing our Schools*. Buckingham: Open University Press.

Sullivan, R. (2000) *Learning and Teaching – What Counts?* (www.pdn.asn.au/confs/2000/sullivan.htm) (online October 2001).

Thomas, H. (1985) Perspectives on evaluation. In M. Hughes *et al.* (eds.) *Managing Education: The System and the Institution*. London: Holt, Rinehart & Winston.

Tomlinson, J. (1996) *Inclusive Learning: The Report of the Learning Difficulties and Disabilities Committee*. Coventry: FEFC.

Torrington, D. and Weightman, J. (1993) The culture and ethos of the school. In M. Preedy (ed.) *Managing the Effective School*. London: Open University/Paul Chapman.

Tower Hamlets Local Educational Authority (1994) *Analysis of 1994 GCSE Results*. London: Tower Hamlets.

Townsend, T., Clarke, P. and Ainscow, M. (eds.) (1999) *Third Millennium Schools: A World of Difference in Effectiveness and Improvement*. Rotterdam: Swets & Zeitlinger.

Trentin, G. (1999) What does 'using the Internet for education' mean? *Educational Technology* July–August: 15–23.

TTA (1998) *National Standards for Subject Leaders*. London: Teacher Training Agency.

Wagner, K. (2000) Management system for a learner centred school. *Educational Management and Administration* 28(4): 373–87.

Wallace, M. and Hall, V. (1994) *Inside the SMT: Teamwork in Secondary School Management*. London: Paul Chapman.

Wang, M.C., Haertel, G.D. and Walberg, H.J. (1997) Learning influences. In H.J. Walberg and G.D. Haertel (eds.) *Psychology and Educational Practice*. Berkeley, CA: McCutchan.

Warwick, D. (1989) Interpretation and aims. In D. Warwick (ed.) *Linking Schools and Industry*. Oxford: Blackwell.

Watkins, D. (2000) Learning and teaching: a cross-cultural perspective. *School Leadership and Management* 20(2): 161–73.

Watkins, D. and Biggs, J.B. (eds.) (1996) *The Chinese Learner: Cultural, Psychological and Contextual Influences*. Hong Kong/Melbourne: Comparative Education Research Centre/Australian Council for Educational Research.

Watts, A.G. (1991) Some international comparisons. In A. Miller *et al.* (eds.) *Rethinking Work Experience*. London: Falmer Press.

Whitaker, P. (1993) *Managing Change in Schools*. Buckingham: Open University Press.

Wise, C.S. (1999) The role of academic middle managers in secondary schools. Unpublished PhD thesis, University of Leicester.

Wong, E.K.P., Sharpe, F.G. and McCormick, J. (1998) Factors affecting the perceived effectiveness of planning in Hong Kong self-managing schools. *Educational Management and Administration* 26(1): 67–81.

Woodhead, M. (1999) 'Quality' in early childhood programmes – a contextually appropriate approach. In B. Moon and P. Murphy (eds.) *Curriculum in Context*. London: Open University/Paul Chapman.

World Bank Group (2000) *Public Examination Systems – Equity* (www1.worldbank.org/education/exams/equity/) (online October 2001).

Yair, G. (1997) When classrooms matter: implications of between-classroom variability for educational policy in Israel. *Assessment in Education* 4(2): 225–48.

Yale University Library (2000) *Pedagogical and Androgogical Approaches to Teaching and Learning* (www.library.yale.edu/training/stod/approaches.htm) (online October 2001).

Author Index

Subject Index